TIMELENGTH
EXHIBITION CATALOG

TIMELENGTH
CATALOGUE DE L'EXPOSITION

GALERIE LEONARD & BINA ELLEN ART GALLERY

JEROEN DE RIJKE/
WILLEM DE ROOIJ
PASCAL GRANDMAISON
GWEN MACGREGOR
JOCELYN ROBERT
MICHAEL SNOW
ANDY WARHOL

COMMISSAIRE
MICHÈLE THÉRIAULT

CONTENTS

PREFACE 4

IMAGES OF AN ITINERARY 8

MATERIALITIES OF DURATION :
Michèle Thériault 28

FILMIC TIME IN INSTALLATION :
Stefan Jovanovič 44

WORKS 64

COMMENTARIES
Gwen MacGregor 98
Jocelyn Robert 98
Michael Snow 99

THOUGHTS ON "EXHIBITION CINEMA" :
Michèle Thériault 104

BIOGRAPHIES 115
LIST OF WORKS 118

SOMMAIRE

PRÉFACE 6

PARCOURS EN IMAGES 8

LES MATÉRIALITÉS DE LA DURÉE :
Michèle Thériault 36

LE TEMPS FILMIQUE DANS L'INSTALLATION :
Stefan Jovanovič 54

OEUVRES 64

COMMENTAIRES
Gwen MacGregor 98
Jocelyn Robert 98
Michael Snow 99

QUELQUES RÉFLEXIONS SUR LE « CINÉMA D'EXPOSITION » :
Michèle Thériault 109

BIOGRAPHIES 116
LISTES DES OEUVRES 118

PREFACE

Michèle Thériault

The exhibition *Timelength* marks a new beginning for the Gallery. Its programming will now focus more intensely on contemporary issues. The mandate of the Gallery has been modified so as to integrate Canadian and Québécois art within an international context. The decision to broaden our field of interest is a signal that it is no longer possible for a university gallery to program outside the international sphere. The public at large, the student population and the artistic community will be the first to benefit from this realignment. However, our commitment to contemporary debate does not signify that we will no longer present exhibitions of a historical nature, but that they will now have to be developed within the perspective of a contemporary problematic.

The presence of the moving and projected image has become a common feature of numerous exhibitions of contemporary art. *Timelength* looks at the moving image from the viewpoint of duration and in relation to different modes of production and presentation. The image in this exhibition, however, is marked by slowness, quasi-fixedness and the play of its opposite, and the circumspect use of sound and silence. The works in video and film by Jeroen de Rijke and Willem de Rooij, Pascal Grandmaison, Gwen MacGregor and Jocelyn Robert are brought into a dialogue with the films of Michael Snow and Andy Warhol, two artists who have transformed the notion of duration in the cinematic image since the sixties. Their works function as referential marks that position the framework of discussion in a recent past. The exhibition also examines how the apprehension of the moving image within a darkened space illuminated by the image alone transforms our relationship to art.

This publication was conceived as a way of extending through writing the discussion on the temporal experience afforded by the films and videos in the exhibition. It brings together two essays by the curator and one by Stefan Jovanovič that examines filmic time in installation. Artists have also contributed commentaries. The catalogue was conceived by Uniform and it is discriminating in the links it forges between the works, the concerns the exhibition addresses, and graphic design.

Timelength poses a challenge to the Gallery's exhibition space. Although designed a little more than ten years ago, it was never conceived so as to accommodate the moving image and sound in the way they have been integrated to artistic practice today. The space had to be reorganized to present large-scale video and film projections. In this respect the curatorial challenge is multifaceted: one has to think through the layout of the works and the relationship between them in relation to a visitor's experience that now takes place entirely in the dark. One can't simply close off spaces, isolate the work, and shut out the light. Darkness, sound and silence must become active components rather than effects in the exhibition's spatial layout and in the visitor's experience. In this way a dialogue can develop between the works and with the viewer, who must be encouraged to inhabit a half-darkened space where the incongruity of the intimate and the public is played out.

PRÉFACE

Michèle Thériault

L'exposition *Timelength* marque un nouveau départ pour la Galerie. Effectivement à compter de l'automne 2004 la Galerie Leonard et Bina Ellen réoriente ses activités vers le contemporain. Le mandat de la Galerie a été modifié de manière à inscrire l'art québécois et canadien dans un contexte international. En élargissant le contexte de présentation de l'art d'ici pour qu'il puisse dialoguer avec l'art d'ailleurs, nous reconnaissons qu'il n'est plus possible aujourd'hui, pour une galerie universitaire, d'élaborer une programmation à l'écart de l'activité artistique internationale. Le grand public, les étudiants de l'université et la communauté artistique n'en seront que mieux servis. Notre engagement dans le débat contemporain ne signifie pas que nous renonçons aux projets à caractère historique, mais ils devront dorénavant être réalisés dans une optique contemporaine et pouvoir éclairer des problématiques actuelles.

La présence de l'image animée et projetée est devenue un lieu commun dans un grand nombre d'expositions d'art contemporain. *Timelength* propose une réflexion sur l'image en mouvement à partir de la notion de durée en rapport avec des modes de production et de présentation différents. Cette image, cependant, est marquée par la lenteur, la quasi-fixité et le jeu avec son contraire, et l'usage circonspect du son et du silence. Le travail en vidéo et en film des artistes Jeroen de Rijke et Willem de Rooij, Pascal Grandmaison, Gwen MacGregor et Jocelyn Robert est mis en relation avec des films de Michael Snow et d'Andy Warhol qui ont tous deux repensé, dès les années soixante, la notion de durée dans l'image filmique. Leurs œuvres fonctionnent tels des indices de référence qui élargissent le champ de réflexion en l'inscrivant dans un passé récent. L'exposition examine également l'appréhension de l'œuvre d'art animée qui se fait dans une obscurité illuminée par l'image seule et qui transforme notre rapport à l'œuvre.

Cet ouvrage a été pensé afin de prolonger la réflexion de l'expérience temporelle des vidéos et des films de l'exposition dans l'écrit. Il regroupe deux essais de la commissaire et un essai de Stefan Jovanovič, qui nous entretient du temps filmique dans l'installation. On y retrouve aussi des commentaires d'artistes. Le catalogue est une conception d'Uniform et c'est avec discernement qu'ils ont tissés des liens entre les œuvres, le propos de l'exposition et le design graphique.

La présentation de *Timelength* a posé un défi. Au moment de la conception de l'espace il y une dizaine d'années, l'image animée et le son n'avaient pas l'importance qu'ils ont aujourd'hui dans la pratique de l'art. Il a donc fallu réaménager l'espace en conséquence. Pour une commissaire le défi se situe à plusieurs niveaux : il faut réfléchir au parcours de l'exposition, au rapport entre des œuvres qui sont maintenant appréhendées dans l'obscurité et au déplacement du visiteur dans ce contexte. On ne peut simplement fermer les espaces, isoler les œuvres et supprimer la lumière. Il faut plutôt envisager l'obscurité, le son et le silence comme des composantes à part entière de la spatialisation de l'exposition et de l'expérience du visiteur, et non pas comme de simples effets. C'est ainsi que les œuvres pourront mieux dialoguer entre elles et avec le visiteur qui doit être amené à s'inscrire dans ce lieu semi-obscur où se joue l'incongruité de l'intime et du public.

IMAGE
ANITIN
PARCO
EN IMA

S OF
ERARY
URS
GES

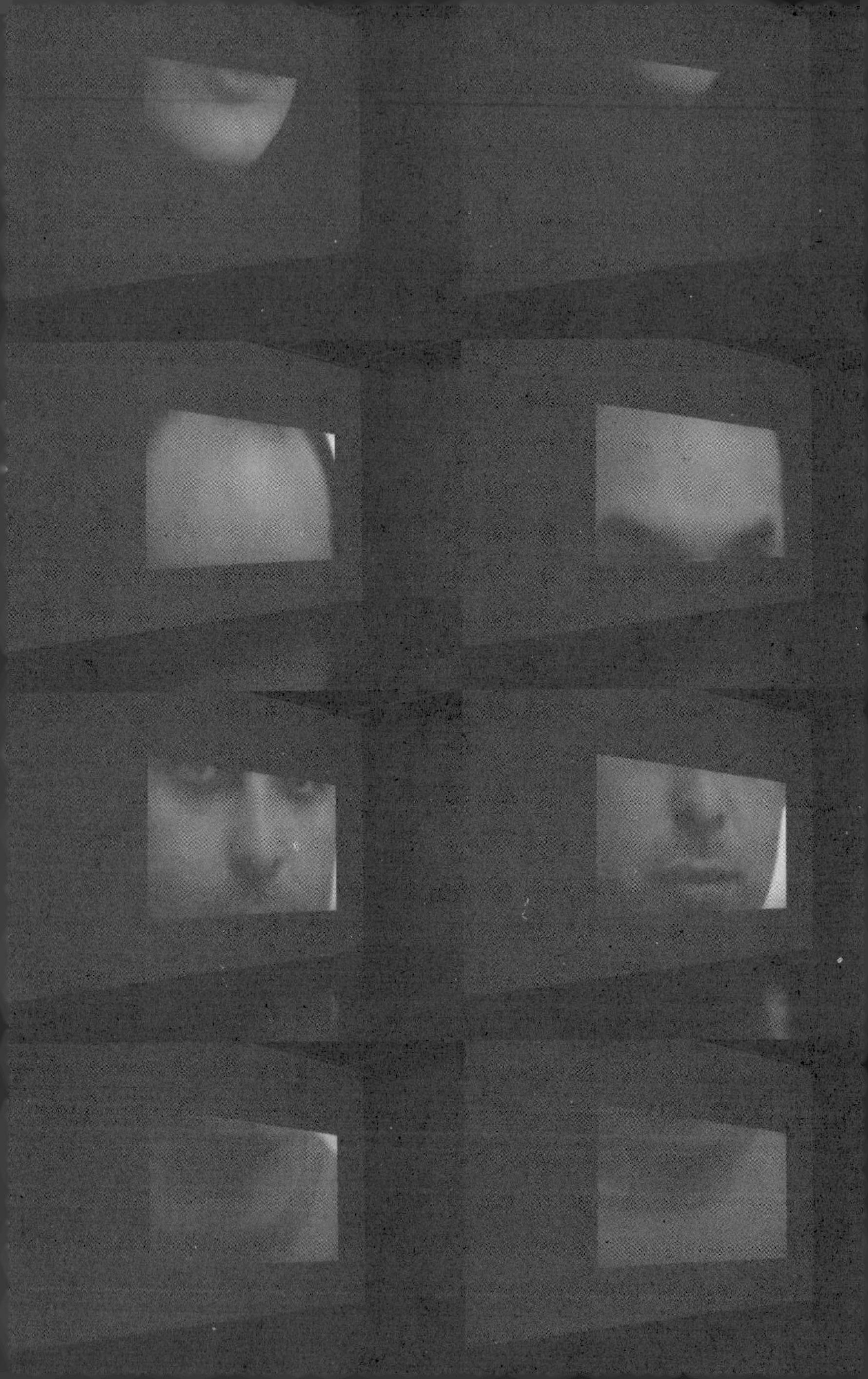

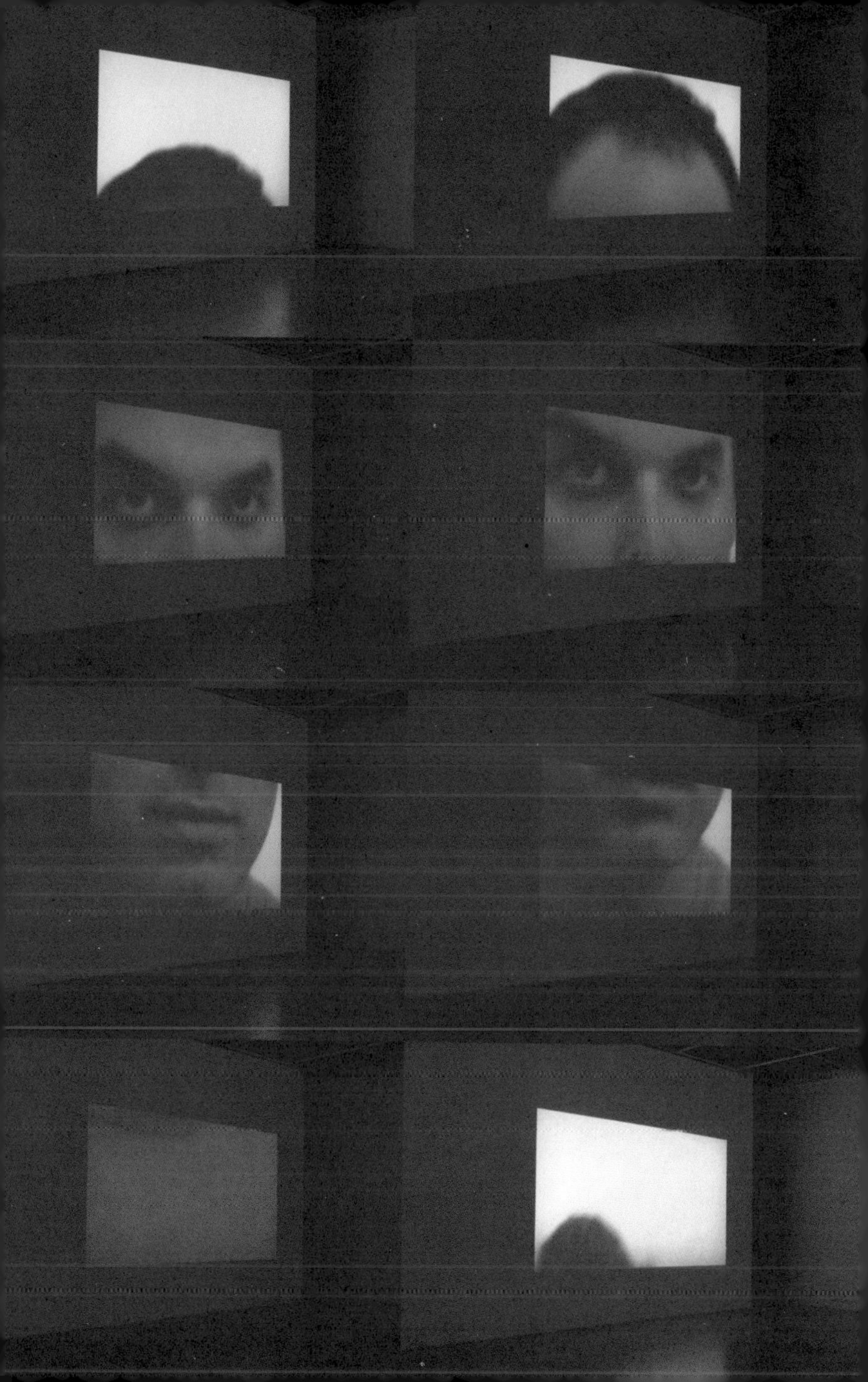

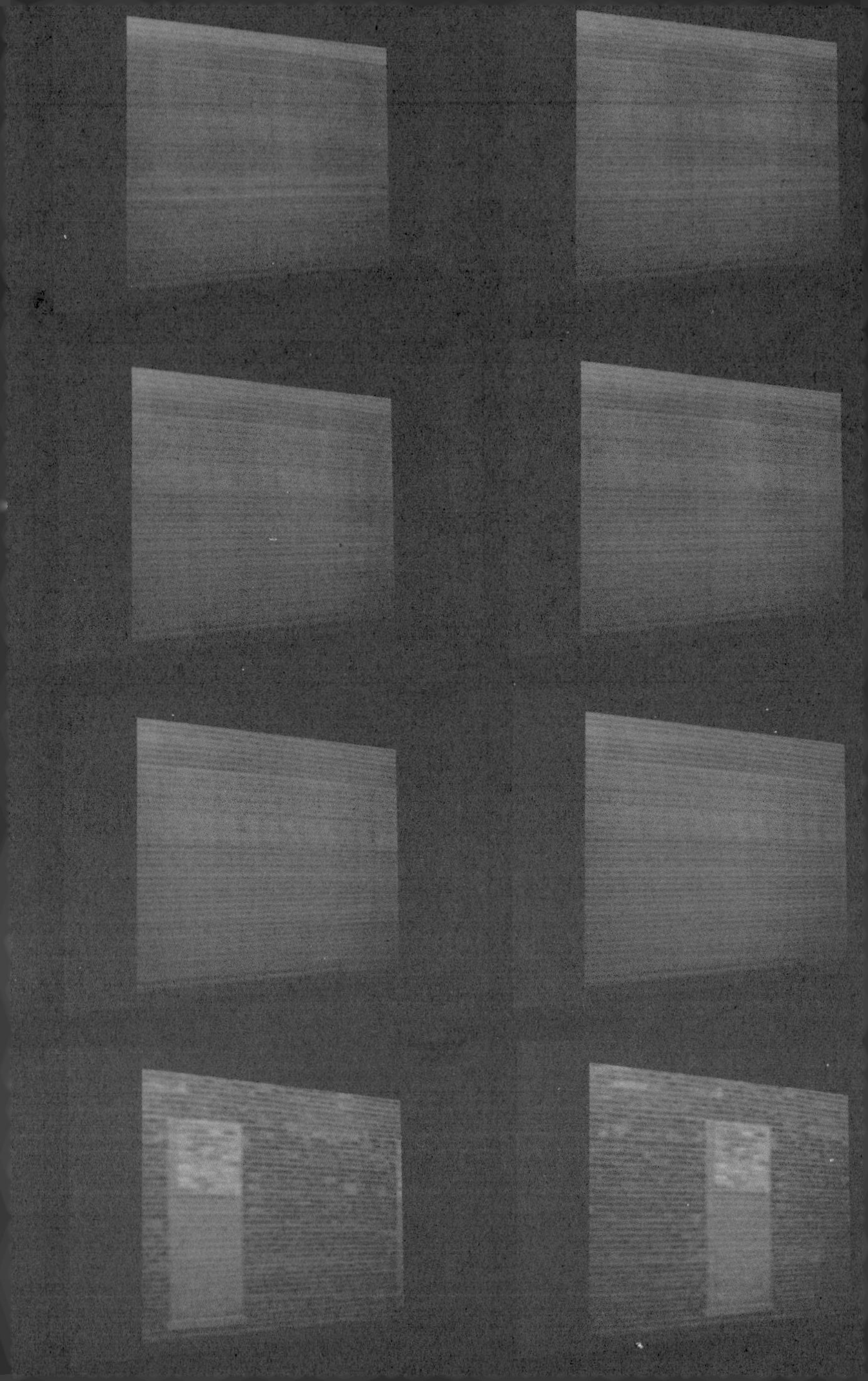

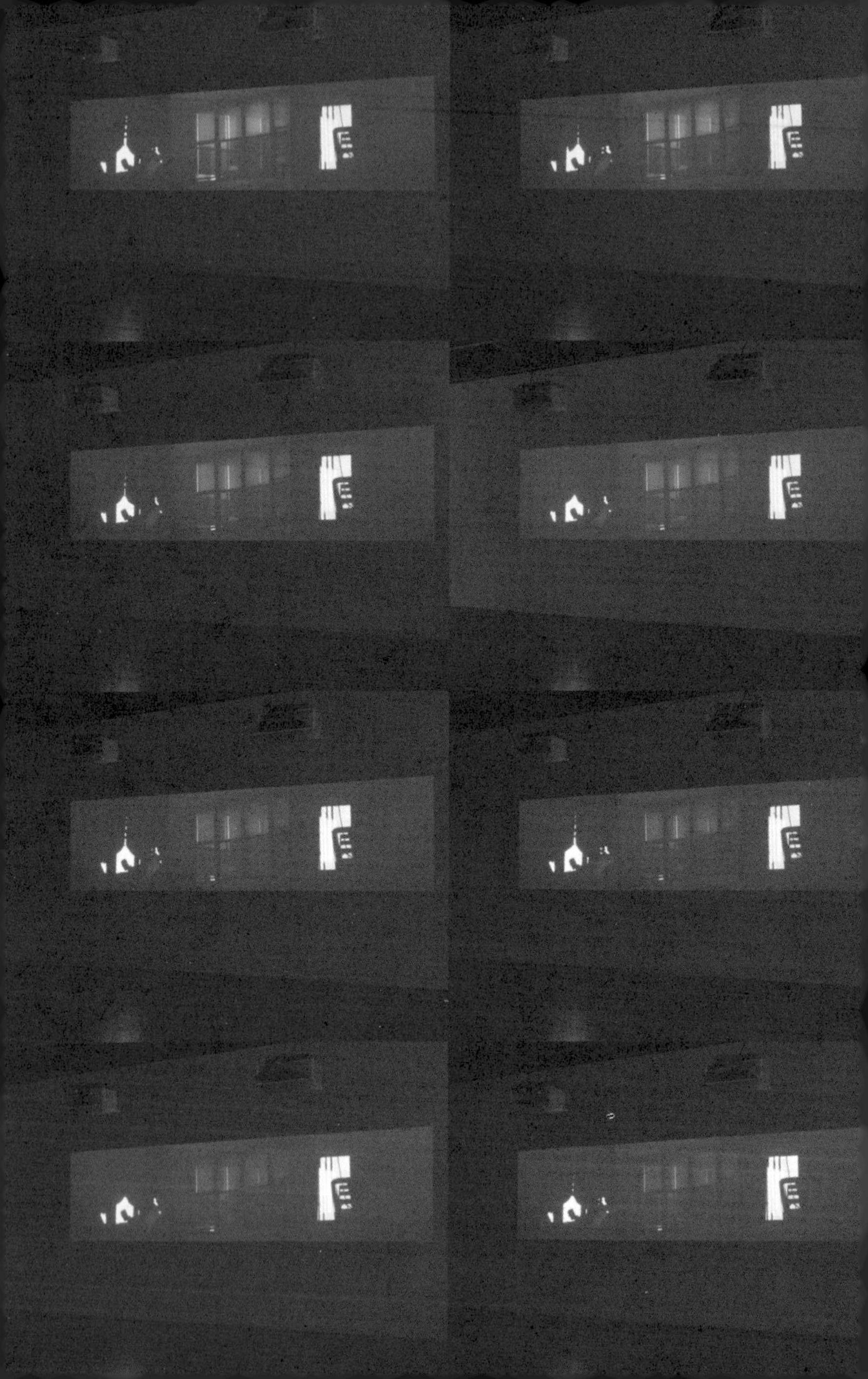

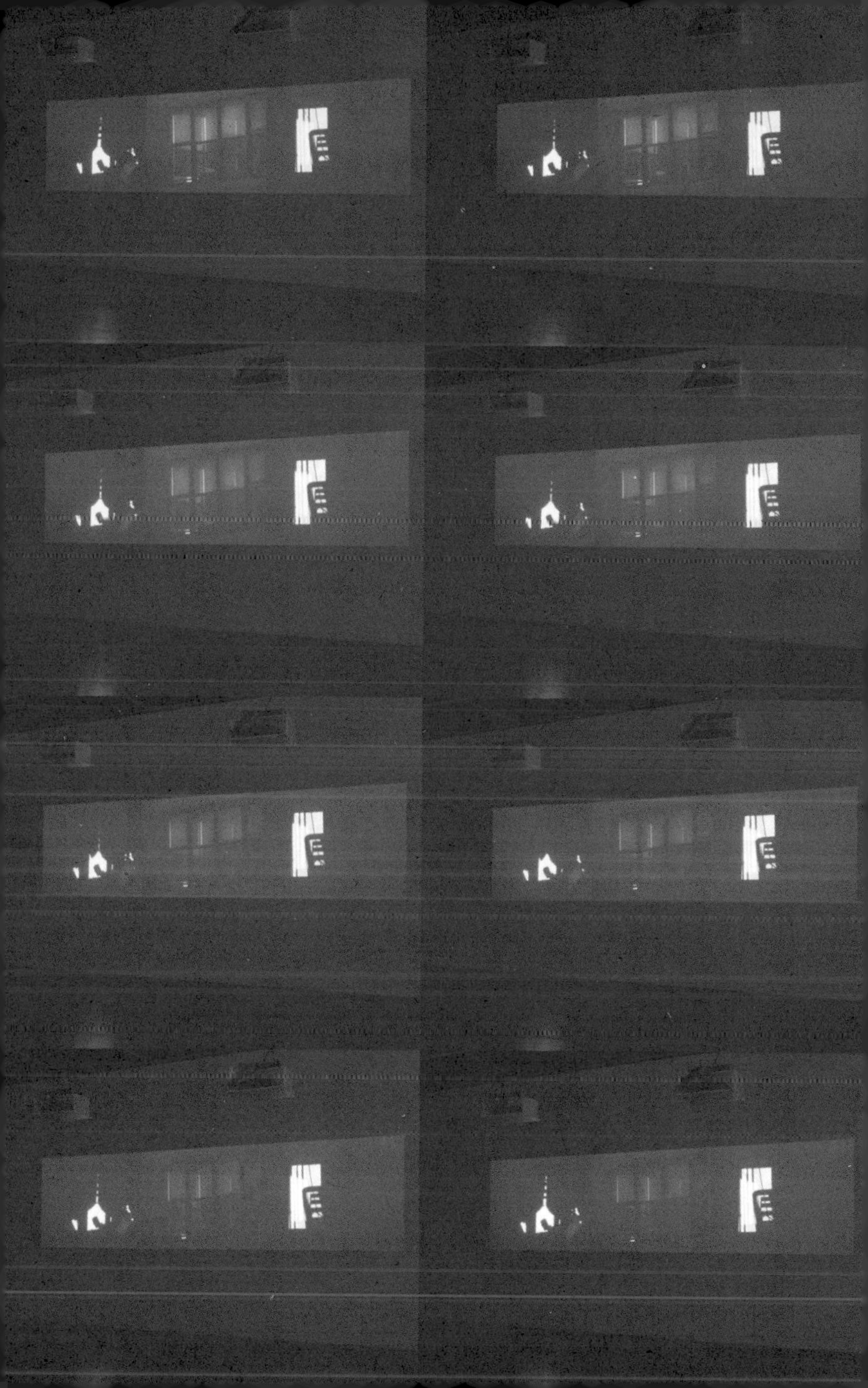

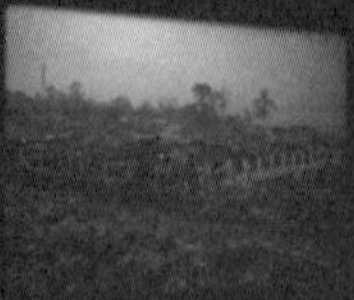
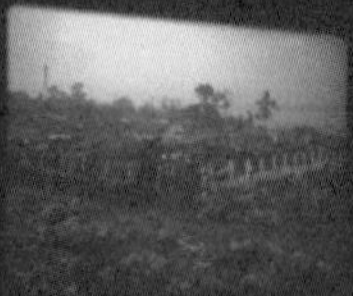
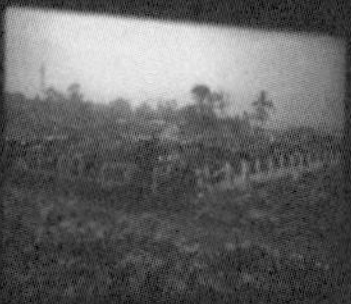
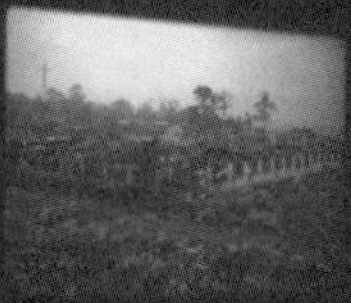
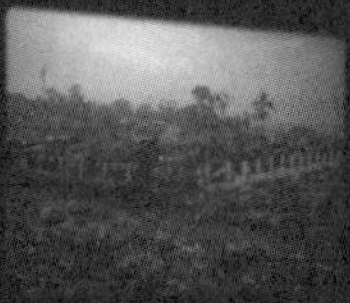
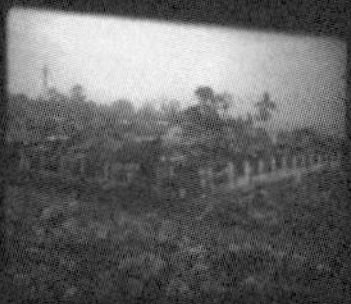
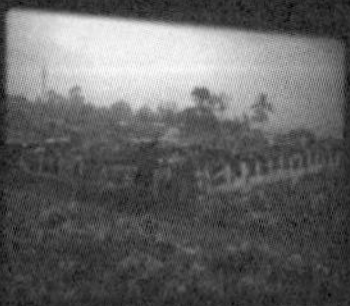
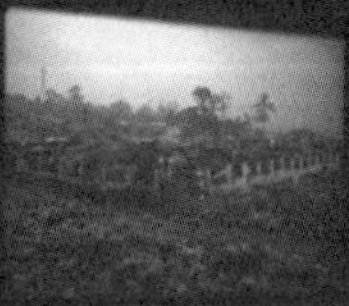

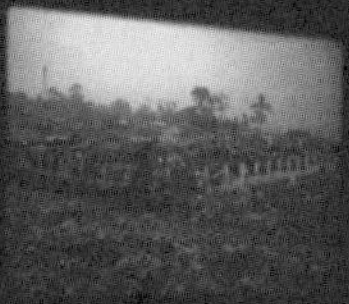
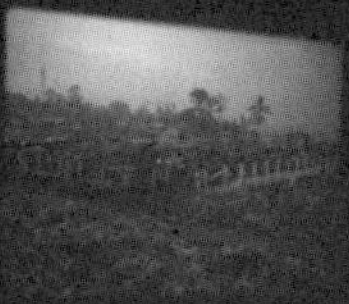
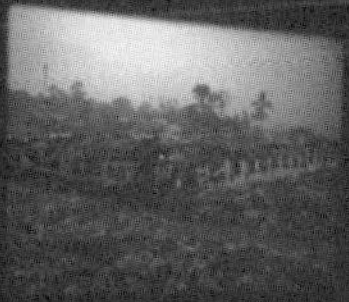
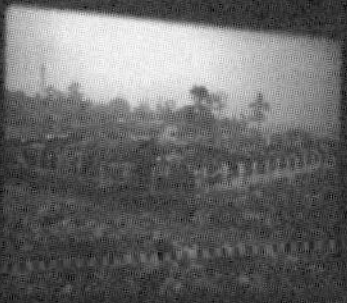
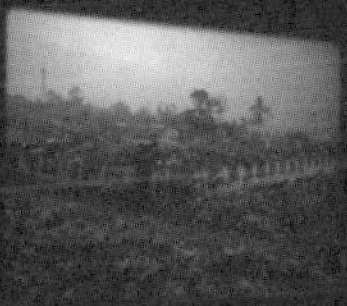
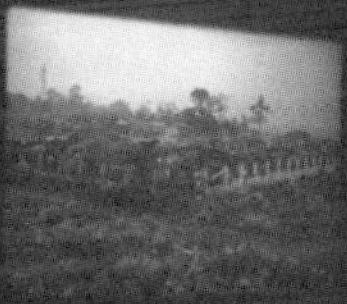
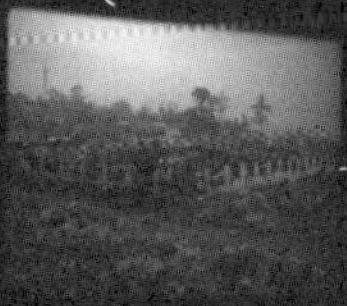
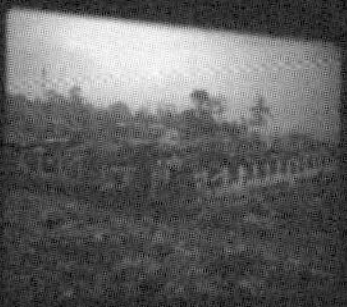

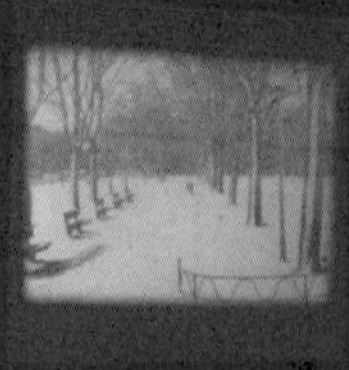
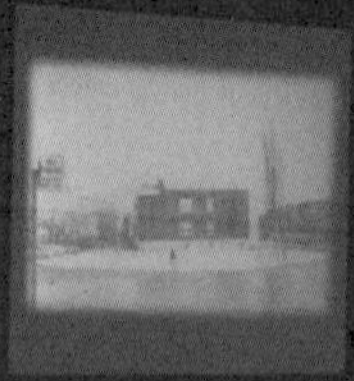
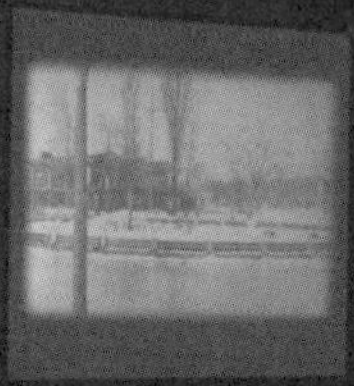
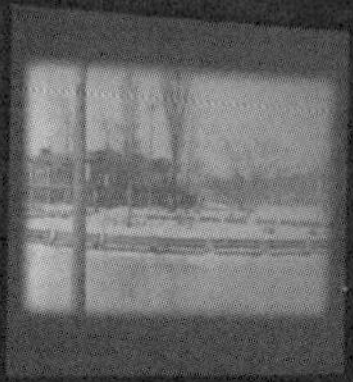
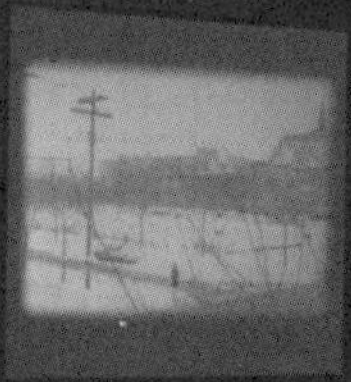
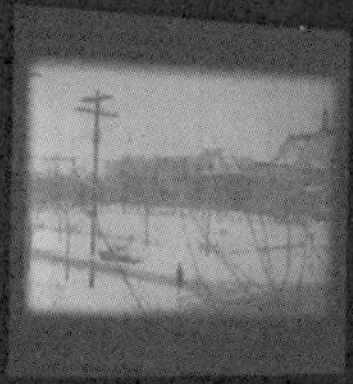
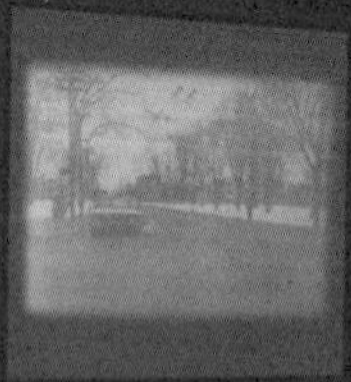
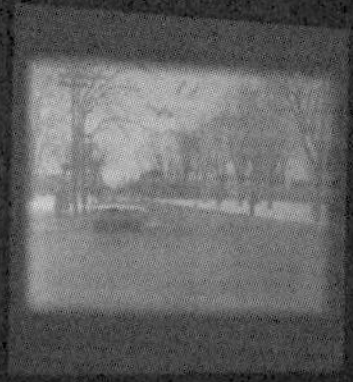

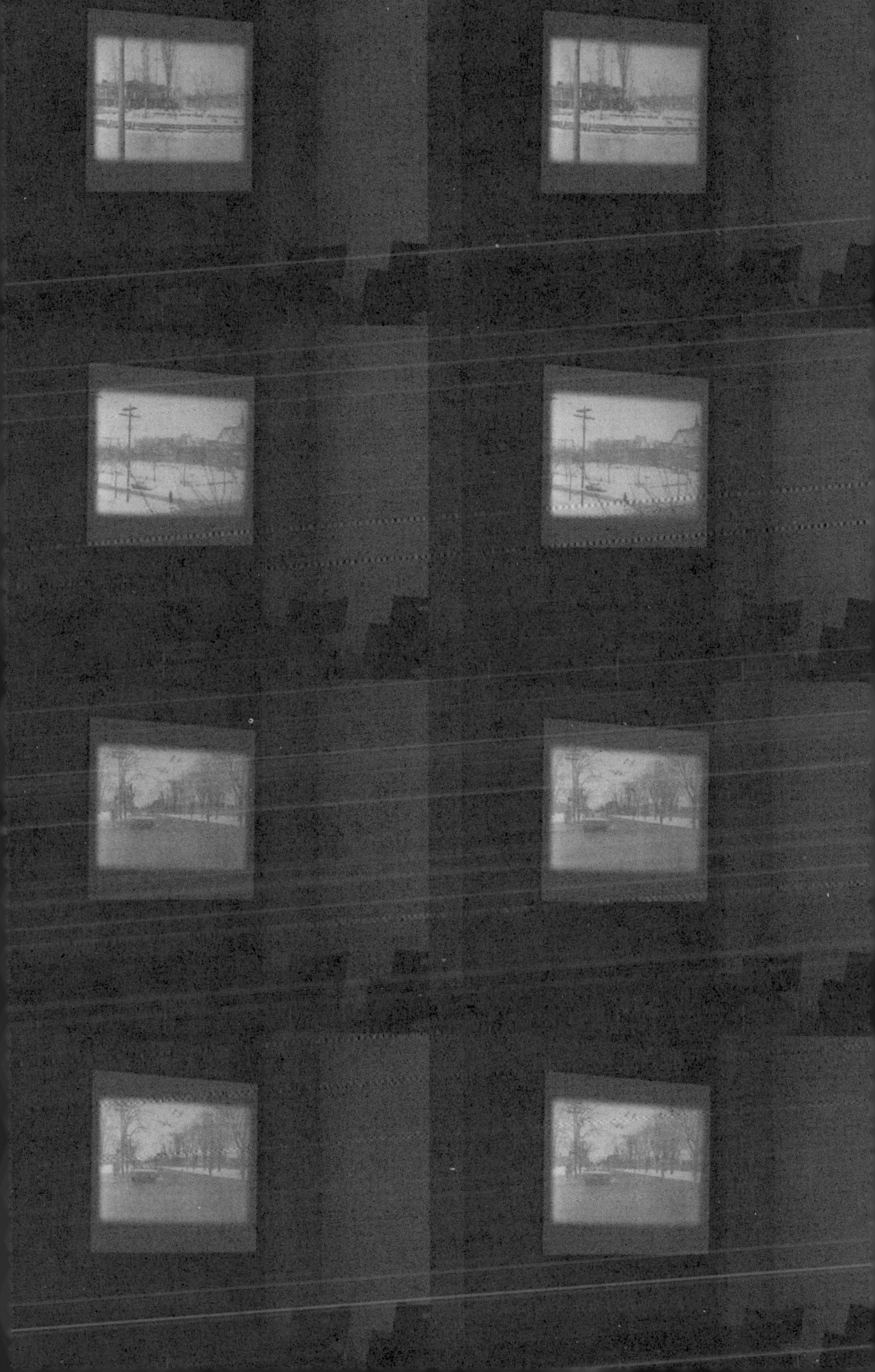

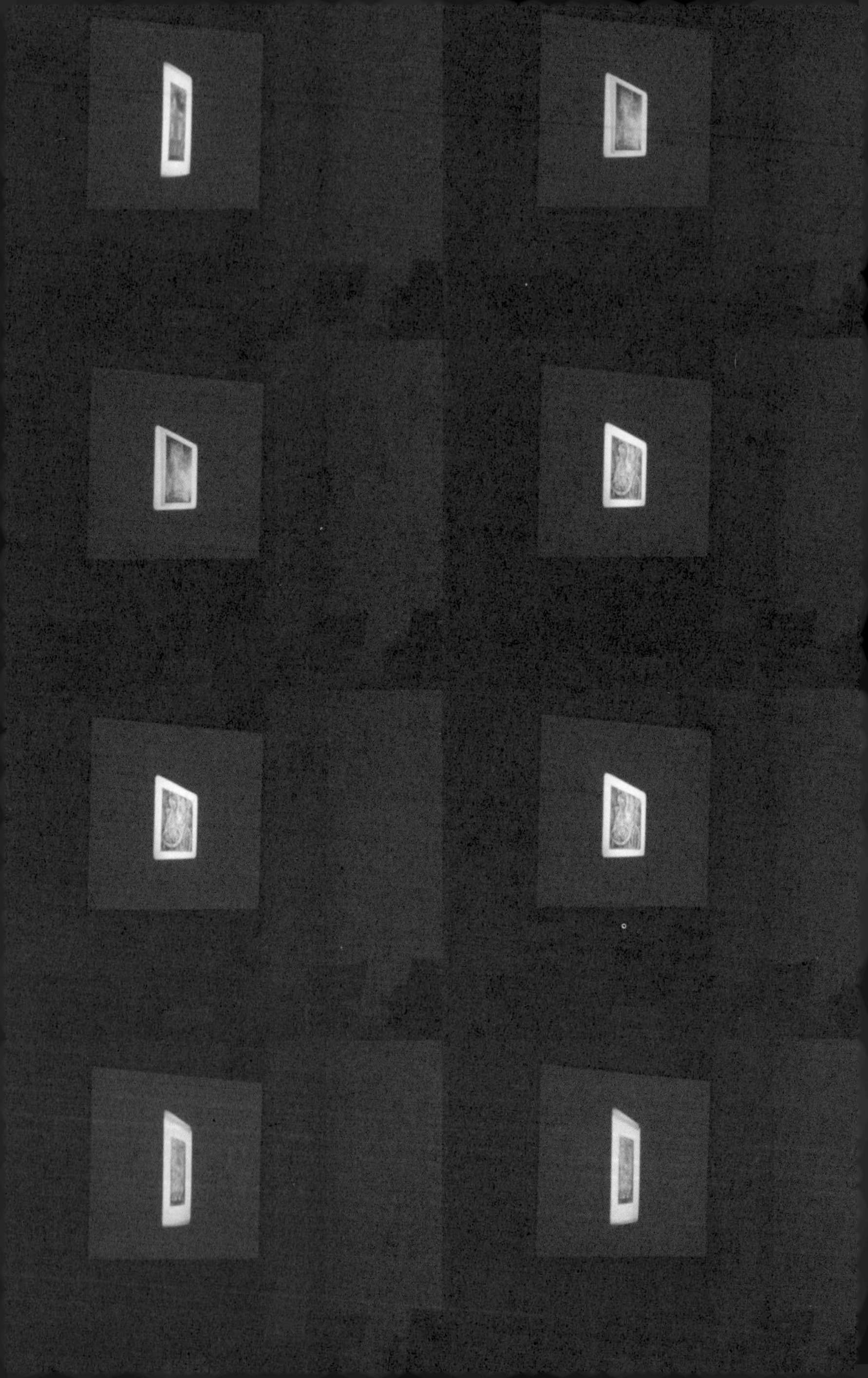

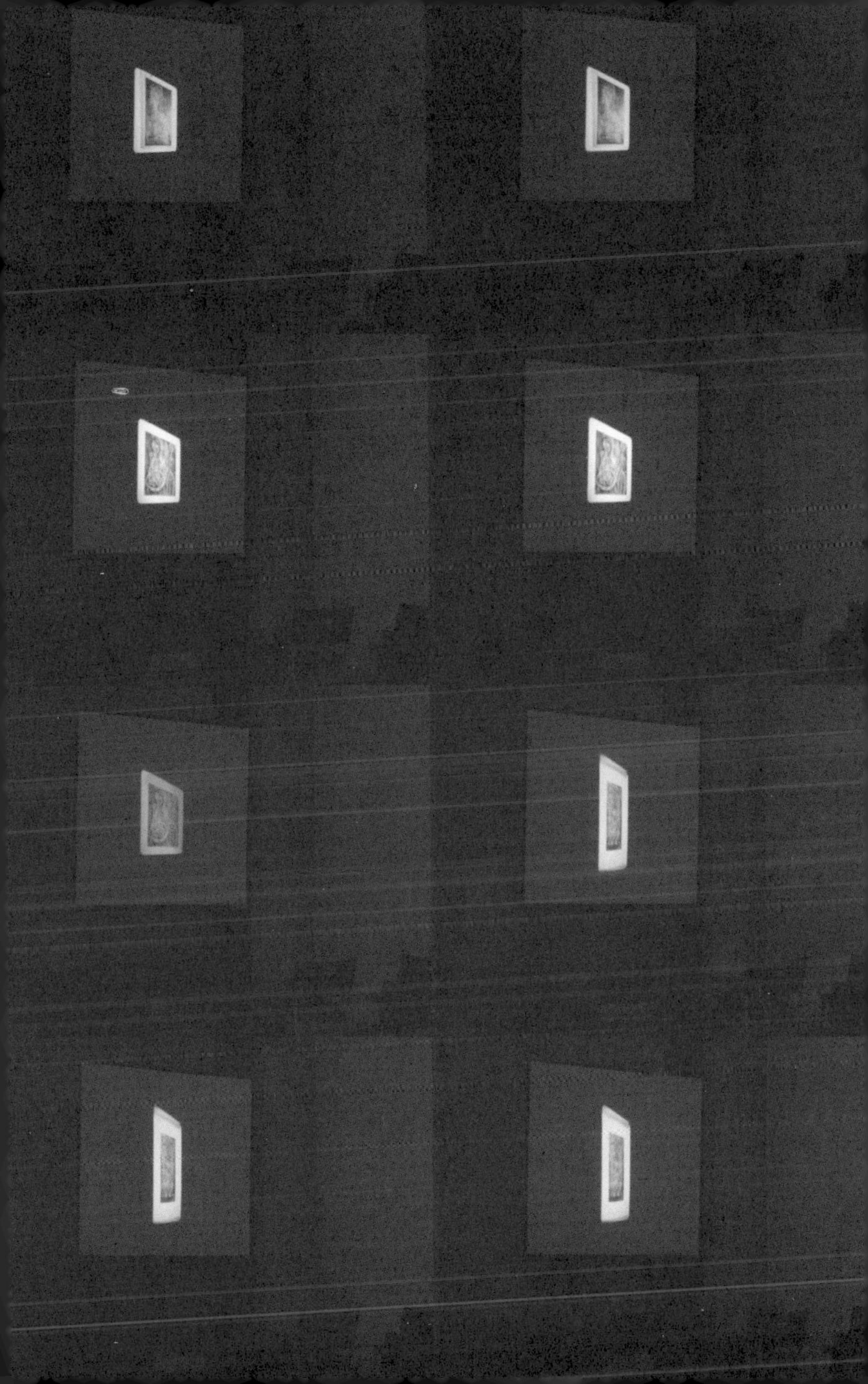

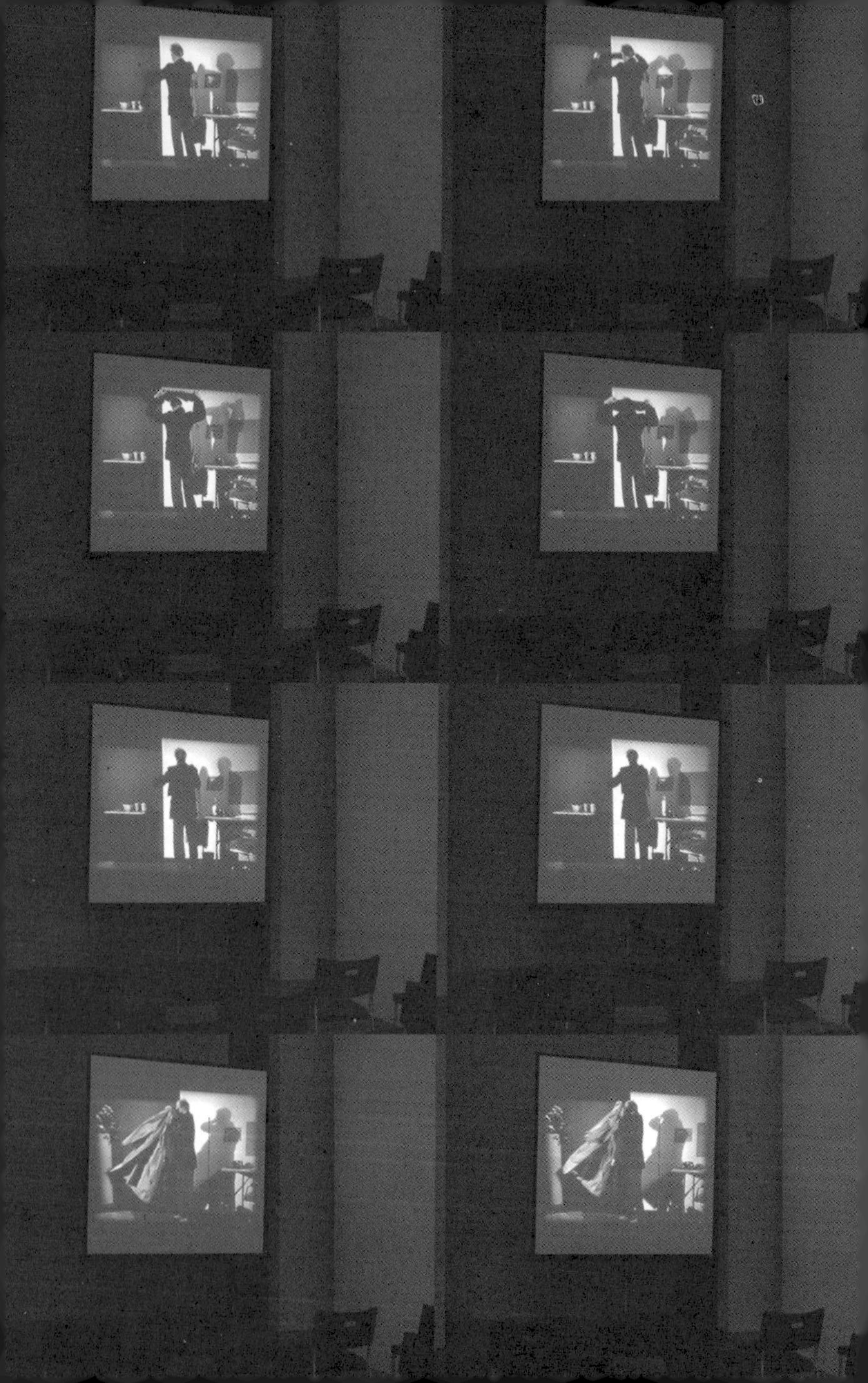

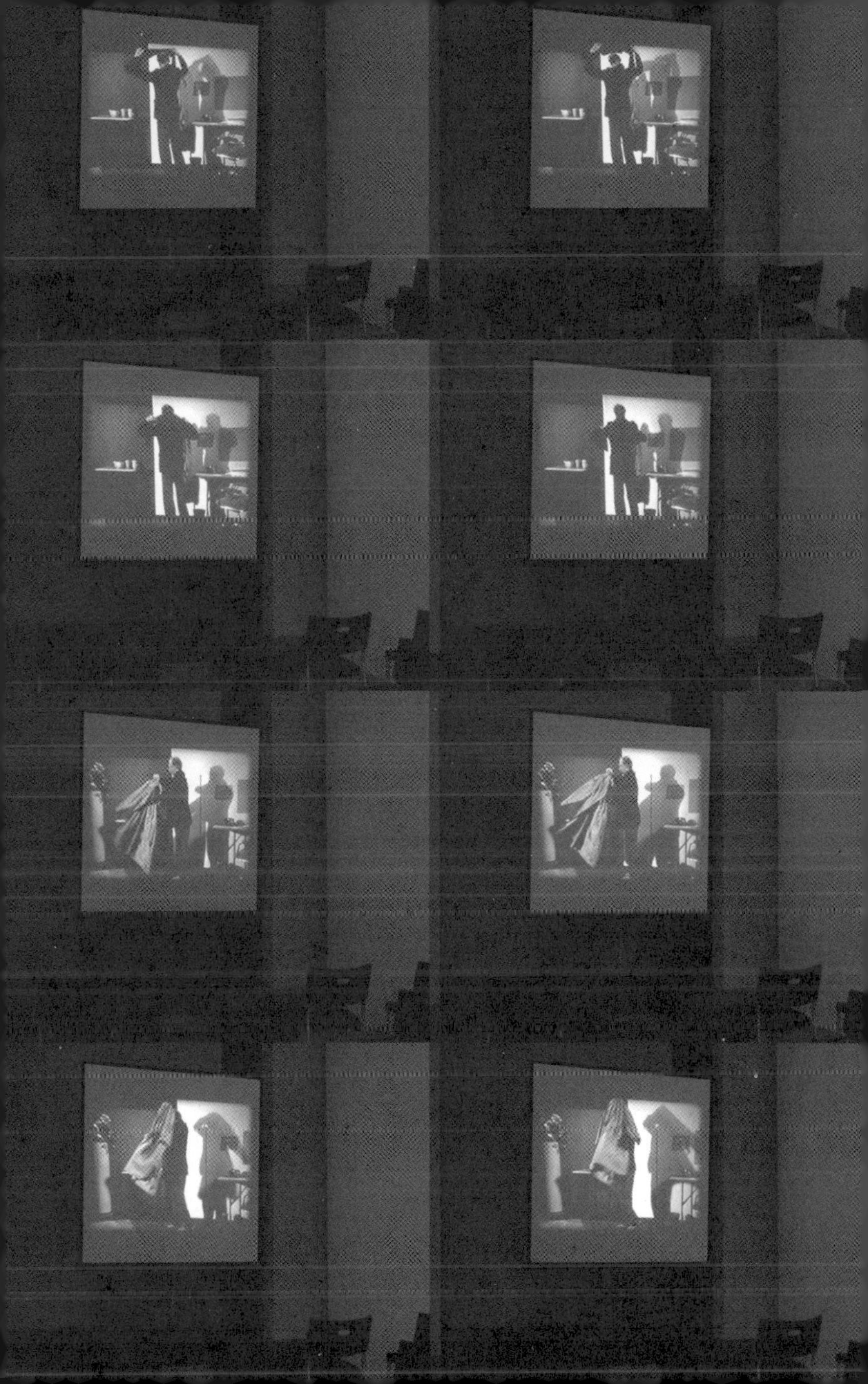

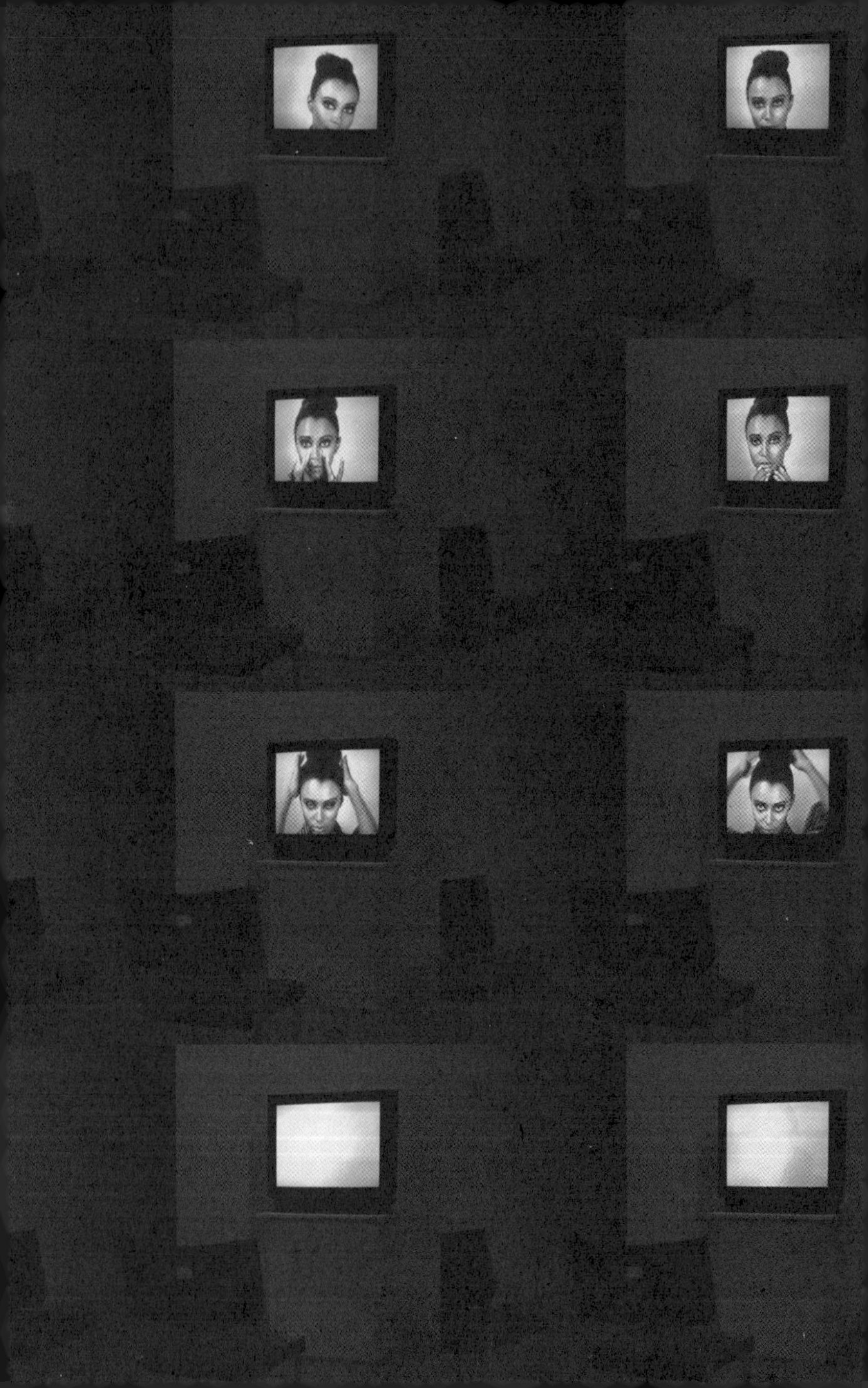

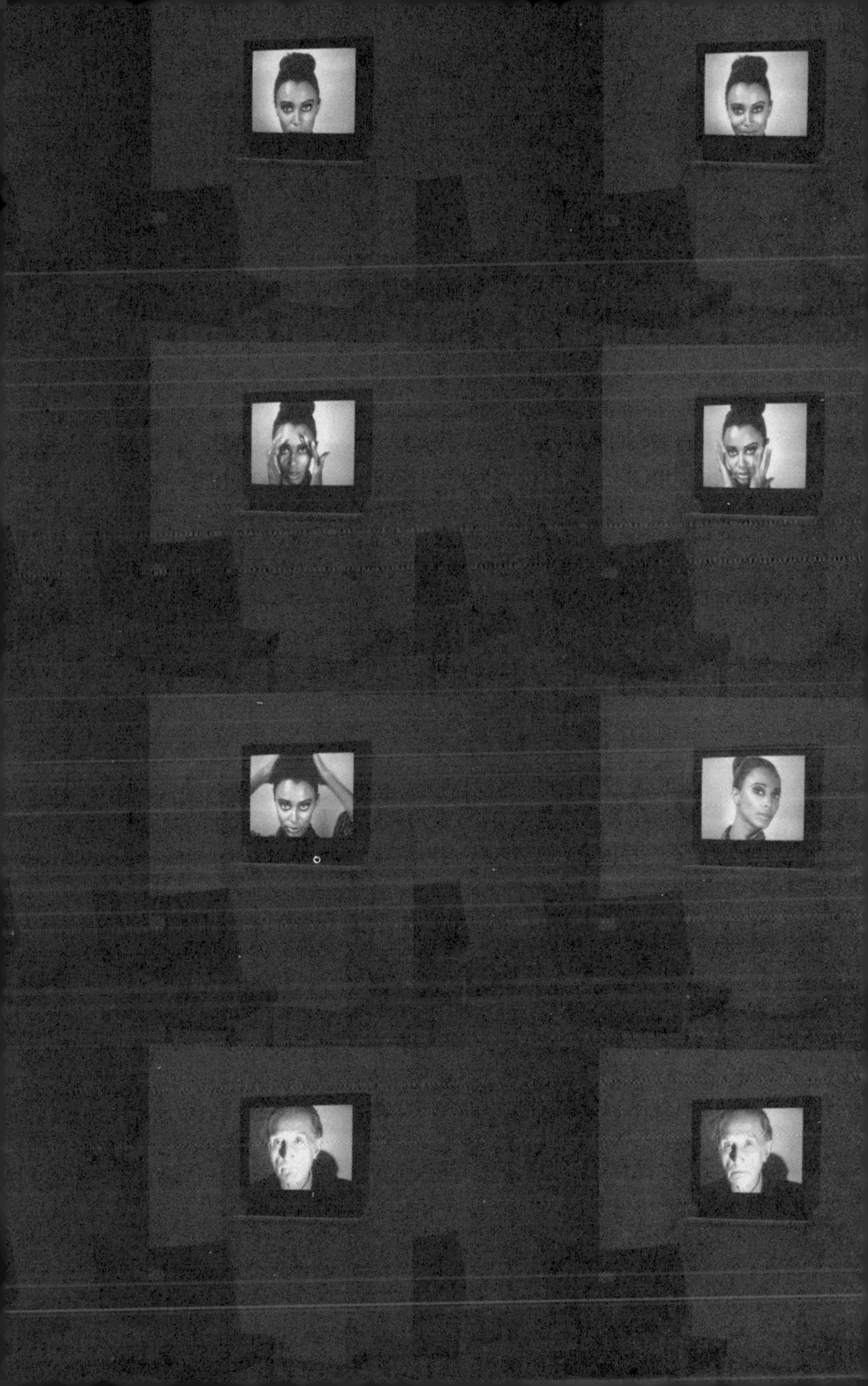

MATERIALITIES OF DURATION

Michèle Thériault

Movement, pause, waiting, mobility, stasis, silence, sound, darkness, light. Works whose effects, in their continued interplay, create duration that takes shape somewhere between temporality and atemporality.

EVENTS OF DURATION

From the moment it becomes the focus of an act of cognition, duration is assimilated to one or more personal experiences. It becomes a state that can be experienced through the cinematographic, literary or pictorial fields, to name but a few. I am thinking here of the temporal commitment that Rober Racine's *Pages-Miroir* and the work of Arakawa and Opalka represent; of Michael Snow's film *Wavelength*, Antonioni's trilogy or Aleksandr Sokurov's *Russian Ark*. In literature there is, of course, the *langueur* of Proust's search, the constitution of duration as entity and its confinement within a logic of circularity in Beckett's œuvre, and the extended time (simultaneously achronological and painstakingly chronological) that runs through the fantastic and troubling tales of Haruki Murakami. These durations, emerging from the construction of parallel and imaginary realities, are incisive openings to duration in the form of durational events, a form that casts duration, so to speak, outside temporality. Like the works brought together in *Timelength,* they place us before a pronounced instance of duration.

The videos of Grandmaison, MacGregor and Robert, and the films of Snow, de Rijke/de Rooij and Warhol (shown here on DVD), were brought together because they materialize duration through a range of registers that enable them to carry on a dialogue with one another, and to draw visitors into a singular experience of duration. Existing only within a darkness penetrated by the light that carries the image, this duration is materialized in the image's prolongation, its slowed movement and its regulated stillness, as well as through the discreet use of sound or silence, which produces a *protracted* time within the viewer, a sense of time that can persist by way of inattention and boredom. A duration, in short, that is the event in itself.

EXCESS

Duration is inextricably tied up with the living being who, although bound to it, remains paradoxically unaware of it. Only when duration intrudes violently upon one's being, when it presents itself as an excess, only then does it become visible and its manifestations can take the form of profound boredom, suffering or joy. Duration's features may be irregular and uneven or indistinct and rooted in repetition. The registers through which the works in *Timelength* operate are marked by excess: the deliberate slowness of the image, hesitant and faltering in *Spin* (2002)*;* or its fixedness rendered by the subjects in the *Screen Tests* (1963-1965) or by the insistent holds on each location shot in *One Second in Montreal* (1969). The subtle and delicate implacability of the transformation of the image and its ambient sound in *Bantar Gebang* (2000) and the abrupt interruptions of narrative flow in the voice in *Catarina (2002*) are, for their part, excess-effects that lead to an extension of sight and hearing – effects that are felt more intensely through the insertion of a subtle interplay between slow motion and acceleration in MacGregor's *Up to the 8th floor* (2004), Robert's *Catarina*, and Snow's *Side Seat Slides Paintings Sound Film* (1970). Each of these works places the viewer before a durational image (or a series of durational images through, for instance, Snow's different holds on each photograph in *One Second in Montreal*) that inscribes its presence outside the boundaries of linear time. Each one does not therefore *represent* duration; it is duration.

MARKING TIME

Our relationship with these works is grounded in the condition of waiting. And because we are dealing with images in motion and technologies of motion, this paradoxical condition which is bound up with slowness, apparent stillness and an interplay with its opposites is sensed in a much more acute fashion. Marking time is experienced through an excess that makes duration manifest. As soon as the eye or ear comes into contact with one of these works, one enters into a condition in which a pronounced sense of waiting becomes an integral part of the optical and acoustic structure. Curious, painstaking, scrutinizing, riveting, encompassing, weighty and even boring – waiting is conjugated in all these ways. It binds vision to the act of scrutinizing and has the effect of making being present to itself. In some cases, particularly in *One Second in Montreal*, *Up to the 8th floor*, *Bantar Gebang* and *Screen Tests*, the process of marking time intrudes upon experience to such an extent that the mind drifts, abandons the work, to then come back to it temporarily, only to leave it again, thereby plunging the viewer into a syncopated duration invaded momentarily by unrelated, everyday thoughts.

WAITING PAUSE MOVEMENT STASIS

Waiting is constituted through the opposition movement/pause and movement/stasis which is played out along the axis of this exhibition. This fruitful opposition, in its shifts between polar extremes, articulates different facets of the exhibition and creates temporal reverberations that also constitute a common material duration. A certain rhythm marks the visitors' movements in the space. Viewers walk, stop, sit, wait and walk again, are detained, waylaid and pushed away from a work, move again and feel this movement reduced to a state of stasis, before freeing themselves from it and moving elsewhere. Accentuated through the works, this rhythm becomes, as it were, the connective tissue linking one durational event to another and the basis for one's experience of it. Consider the interplay of movement and stasis in *Up to the 8th floor* and *Catarina*: the viewer will simultaneously find him or herself grappling with the body's mobility and the work as the image's speed shifts back and forth. Consider how one's gaze and body is locked into the unrelenting hold of the image when the projection of *Bantar Gebang* begins only to be slowly released as the gestures of daily human existence start to animate the projection's expanse. This rhythm creates not only a regime of viewing in time but of listening, a regime not only of the mind but also of the living body.

DARKNESS INCONGRUITY

All of the activities that take place around the experience of duration unfold through the strange interaction of our bodies in a space that has been plunged into darkness, illuminated only by projections and traversed by ambient sounds that are, at times, difficult to identify (*Bantar Gebang*, *See You Later/Au revoir* [1990]), or by spoken words interrupted or indeed distorted by various processes (*Catarina*, *Side Seat Paintings Slides Sound Film*). This is not quite the cinematic experience described by Roland Barthes, for the freedom to move about as one wishes is much greater, even with the films of Snow and de Rijke/de Rooij which are presented in typical cinema fashion complete with screening times and a projectionist.[1] The experience is more one of exhibition-cinema, of the "black box" type.[2] Walking around, sitting on a bench or on the floor, leaning against the wall, staring at the image, drawing closer to it, scanning the walls of the space and going from room to room in a constant, artificially created semi-darkness, creates a relationship of incongruity with the space and among visitors and a significant rupture between the exhibition and the outside, day-to-day world. The singular circumstances surrounding the perception of space and images in *Timelength* results in a more intimate and, in some ways, captive relationship with a work, and, through it, one can experience a duration that disturbs temporality.

FILM VIDEO PROJECTION MONITOR

Timelength is designed to have visitors experience duration through an excess that is inextricably tied to a process of production, since this profoundly material incursion into time to be apprehended in its density is the product of processes and modes of presentation that are quite distinct from one another: video and film; projectors and monitors; continuous loops and screening times. It was important, therefore, to present both films and videos in their original forms at the gallery. Only Andy Warhol's *Screen Tests*, filmed in 16mm and transferred to DVD, are shown on a monitor. Today we tend to make less and less of a distinction between film and video: some artists film in 35mm format and then transfer the film to digital video format, while a number of experimental filmmakers, like Stan Brakhage, have agreed to let their works be transferred to video. If attention to the differences between these media is warranted then it is because film and video have distinct processes of production and produce images and durations specific to each. *Timelength* is designed to highlight each medium's particular divergences, discrepancies and effects as a function of particular works.

FILM

Timelength presents three 16mm films by Michael Snow (*One Second in Montreal*, *Side Seat Slides Paintings Sound Film* and *See You Later/Au revoir*) and one 35mm film, *Bantar Gebang*, by the Dutch artists Jeroen de Rijke and Willem de Rooij. One can examine, in these cases, how media and presentation constitute duration differently. Since 1994, de Rijke and de Rooij have collaborated on the production of films designed to be shown specifically in galleries or museums. It is worth noting that these artists do not describe themselves as filmmakers, unlike Michael Snow, who is known as an experimental filmmaker, as well as a painter, sculptor and musician. Snow, moreover, usually presents his works in a cinema-like environment.

Bantar Gebang is a 10-minute film shot in 35mm; those of Michael Snow, shot in 16mm, have running times of 26, 20 and 18 minutes respectively. These films are shown at set times in a space set aside specifically for them in the gallery. Visitors are therefore required to be present at the prescribed times if they wish to view the films. They have to take their places and wait for the projectionist to start the film. After some time, let's say 10 or 26 minutes, the image fades to black, the projector is switched off, and visitors get up and leave the room. This process runs counter to the more indeterminate character of the experience associated with video loops. In this case, visitors are free to view the work when they so desire, but they cannot easily determine the point at which they must enter the loop for it might be of no consequence to the work itself. Hence their feeling of being unable to grasp the work in its entirety. With predetermined screening times, such as those set for the films of Snow and de Rijke/de Rooij, the works' starting and finishing points are clearly delineated; the experience of duration begins in those moments of anticipation, before an empty, silent screen registers the first images, and ends with the disappearance of the last image and the switching off of the projector. Moreover, viewing from a seated position, coupled with the physical presence and sound (although muted) of the projector – in short, the whole ritual of projection, its theatricality, so to speak – are an integral part of the experience of these projected film-works. In them, duration operates in three interrelated modes: anticipation in the semi-darkness of the screening room before the projector is switched on; duration through the exact amount of time it takes to show the film; and duration *within* the work itself. Since the films of Snow and de Rijke/de Rooij are durational works – with Snow extending and exposing duration, and de Rijke and de Rooij rendering it implacable in its progressive invasiveness – the duration produced by the apparatus and mode of presentation is constituted within its own *mise en abîme* that projects it even farther outside ordinary time.

TRANSFERS

Andy Warhol's *Screen Tests*, which are presented on a monitor in *Timelength* are originally 4-minute 16mm films, that have been transferred to DVD by The Andy Warhol Museum. These are the only non-projected works in the exhibition, hence the only ones whose relationship with the viewer is, strictly speaking, televisual. Displacement is, therefore, a feature of these films in terms of both the immediate presentation environment and viewing mode. The blurring and cross-contamination of processes and media witnessed in the presentation of these *Screen Tests* make for a more nuanced experience of duration in these 'pieces of film' that can be described as intense moments of duration. We know that Warhol often showed his films in his studio, the Factory, while other activities simultaneously took place. Visitors viewed these films in whatever manner they pleased, and were not required to keep quiet. Duration in each *Screen Test* is constituted, on the one hand, by a person staring at (or being stared at by) the lens, and, on the other, by the viewer's gaze, in turn immobilized, as it were, in the act of observing a head imprisoned by the lens and the framing of the image. In Warhol's studio, however, the surrounding activities would have intruded on the viewer's experience, and one might very well conclude that duration *within* the work was completely evacuated. In a gallery and through a monitor, the experience has a completely different character. The more intimate scale of the monitor creates a sort of bond between our gaze and that of the subject staring at the lens (Ann Buchanan, Billy Name) or performing before it (Walter Dainwood, Donyale Luna). Through the waiting that becomes more concentrated before each *Test*, a duration is created that exists outside of the normal course of things.

Moreover, within the context of *Timelength* and some 40 years after they were made, the *Tests* have become imbued with a lyrical and occasionally melancholic dimension that certainly did not characterize them at the time of their production. All this gives the work a more hieratic quality – but not without a tinge of irony. The transfers the *Tests* have been subjected to echo the very nature of Warhol's work, which engaged complacently with the idea of the copy and deliberately confused notions of authenticity. In this prosaic, televisual relationship with the work and in our distancing from the original mode of production, duration is not entirely synonymous with what emerges from this exercise in banal endurance – staring at the camera lens for several minutes – but also subsists *in* the time of endurance and survival, which has brought these short 'pieces of film' simultaneously here and elsewhere.

VIDEO

In video projections duration exhibits its own set of attributes. Since the ones in this exhibition run in continuous loops, the image is at all times present and accessible (its larger-than human scale acts as a plane of attraction, a field of vision in which viewers can sometimes lose themselves) and duration becomes part of a continuum in space. We are drawn into its orbit and remain suspended there until we wish to leave. Waiting in the works of Grandmaison, MacGregor and Robert occurs only *within* them and since these works embody a quality of marking time, duration takes on an additional sense of materiality. While the 16 or 35mm projection apparatus produces duration through its presence within the field of the work and functions as a historical vector, this is not the case with the video projector, which has a more strictly utilitarian role. Moreover, its relatively recent use in exhibitions and its pervasiveness in museums and galleries deprives it of symbolic value. As soon as they enter the gallery space, viewers 'enter' the image and, in some cases, the soundtrack, and since both run continuously, they pre-exist the visitor's arrival and will continue playing after they have left. In the works of Grandmaison, MacGregor and Robert the presence of duration becomes spatial, even merging with the space at times, and its experience undergoes a kind of stretching out. When duration does change registers, it does so in the carefully calibrated time frame created by the projection of films for set periods of time. Between these two modes of producing and presenting images and sounds, there emerges a duration whose materiality possesses fluctuating contours.

IMAGE SILENCE SOUND BODY

Timelength places us before images that are sometimes multiple and sequential (*Spin*, *Screen Tests*, *One Second in Montreal*), that are inscribed within a narrative sequence (*One Second in Montreal*, *Side Seat*, *See You Later/Au revoir*, *Catarina*) or that constitute a single view that undergoes, nevertheless, numerous subtle transformations within its sequence (*Bantar Gebang*, *Up to the 8th floor*). The image has, of course the power to fascinate and exhibitions that have focused on the projected image have exploited this characteristic. This exhibition, in contrast, does not focus solely on the 'image' or, more precisely, on the unique power of the durational image; rather, it focuses on the image as part of a complex that produces duration, and that includes sound, silence and the body, but also as we have seen earlier, as an image that is linked to specific technologies of presentation. Thus the silence accompanying the works of MacGregor, Grandmaison, Snow's *One Second in Montreal* and Warhol's *Screen Tests*, which is as much an absence of sound as a presence that fills the space, is a component of the materialization of duration within the image and of our experience of this as excess and as a mode of waiting. Sound as accentuated ambient noise in *Bantar Gebang*, as the interrupted flow of the narrative voice in *Catarina*, as a distorted voice in Snow's *Side Seat* and as the tapping of the typewriter keys in *See You Later/Au revoir* continually probes the durational image and scores the process of marking time.

In each case the sound or silence produced activates a listening process, thereby requiring us to use a sense other than sight to determine the parameters of the work. In *Timelength*, the event of duration is experienced in a relationship that weaves together vision, hearing and the body in motion and at rest. *Timelength* is above all a spatialization of works that seeks to highlight the complexity and the subtle divergences and discrepancies in their structures and their modes of presentation that combine to produce the experience of a time that is extended and strangely exceeds temporality.

NOTES

1. Roland Barthes, "Leaving the Movie Theater," in *The Rustle of Language*, Richard Howard trans. (New York: Hill & Wang, 1987), pp. 345-349.

2. There is an ongoing debate on this question, as well as a body of literature devoted to it. See my "Thoughts on Exhibition Cinema" in this catalogue.

LES MATÉRIALITÉS DE LA DURÉE

Michèle Thériault

Mouvement, arrêt, attente, mobilité, stase, silence, son, obscurité, lumière. Œuvres dont les effets dans leur jeu continu créent de la durée qui prend forme quelque part entre la temporalité et l'atemporalité.

ÉVÉNEMENTS-DURÉE

Dès qu'elle fait l'objet d'un acte de cognition la durée se colle à une ou à des expériences personnelles. Elle devient état. La durée peut donc être vécue, entre autres, à travers le champ cinématographique, littéraire ou pictural. Je pense ici au projet de vie que fut la réalisation des *Pages-Miroirs* de Rober Racine, qu'est l'œuvre d'Arakawa et d'Opalka ; au film *Wavelength* de Michael Snow, à la trilogie d'Antonioni ou à *L'Arche russe* d'Alexandre Sokourov. Dans l'écrit, il y a bien sûr la *langueur* de la recherche chez Proust, la durée constituée en entité et emprisonnée dans sa circularité chez Beckett, et un temps long, à la fois achronologique et aux prises avec une chronologie minutieuse, dans les histoires fantastiques, cocasses et troublantes de Haruki Murakami. Ces durées issues de la construction de réalités parallèles et imaginaires, sont des ouvertures incisives à la durée sous la forme d'événements-durée, qui en quelque sorte l'expulse de la temporalité. À la manière des œuvres réunies dans *Timelength,* elles nous mettent en présence marquée de la durée.

Les vidéos de Grandmaison, MacGregor et Robert et les films de Snow, de Rijke/de Rooij, et Warhol (présentés sous format DVD) ont été rassemblés parce qu'ils matérialisent la durée sur différents registres qui leur permet de dialoguer entre eux et d'entraîner le visiteur dans une expérience singulière de celle-ci. Ne pouvant exister que dans l'obscurité traversée par l'illumination de l'image, cette durée se matérialise dans la lenteur du mouvement, la nature réglée de l'image, sa quasi-fixité et l'usage circonspect du son ou du silence qui fait vivre au regardeur un temps *long*, un temps qui *dure* parfois dans l'inattention et l'ennui. Une durée, en somme, qui est événement.

EXCÈS

La durée est inextricablement liée à l'être vivant et bien qu'il soit son prisonnier il en demeure paradoxalement inconscient. Ce n'est que lorsqu'elle le violente, lorsqu'il y a excès, que la durée devient apparente, et sa reconnaissance se décline tant bien dans l'ennui profond que la jouissance et la souffrance. Sa géographie peut être tantôt profondément accidentée, tantôt dépourvue de tout relief et ancrée dans la répétition. Les registres sur lesquels les œuvres jouent de la durée dans *Timelength* sont marqués par l'excès : la lenteur délibérée de l'image ou son ralentissement, hésitant et chancelant dans *Spin* (2002), sa quasi-fixité rendue par les figurants dans les *Screen Tests* (1963-1965) ou par le maintien du plan dans *One Second in Montreal*(1969). La subtile et délicate implacabilité de la transformation de l'image et du son ambiant dans *Bantar Gebang* (2000) et les ruptures abruptes dans le flot du récit de la voix dans *Catarina* (2002) sont à leur tour des effets d'excès menant à un allongement du regard et de l'écoute. Effets ressentis encore plus vivement par l'intercalation d'un jeu-montage subtil entre le ralenti et l'accéléré dans *Up to the 8th floor* (2004) de MacGregor, *Catarina* de Robert et *Side Seat Slides Paintings Sound Film* (1970) de Snow. Chacune des œuvres met le visiteur en présence d'une image-durée (ou une suite d'images-durée comme dans les plans fixes à durée variable dans *One Second in Montreal*) qui trace son périmètre hors du cours du temps linéaire et quotidien. Chacune ne *représente* donc pas la durée, elle *est* durée.

ATTENTE

La mise en attente est à la base de notre rapport avec ces œuvres. Et parce qu'il s'agit d'images en mouvement et de technologies du mouvement cette attente paradoxale liée à la lenteur, à l'apparence de fixité, et le jeu avec son contraire est d'autant plus ressentie. L'attente est vécue dans un excès qui rend la durée manifeste. Dès que le regard et l'ouïe entrent en contact avec l'une d'entre elle, l'attente est présente d'une façon marquée et devient partie prenante de l'enjeu optique et sonore. Curieuse, minutieuse, scrutatrice, sidérée, enveloppante, pesante, voire ennuyeuse, l'attente se décline de toutes ces manières. Elle astreint le regard à une activité de scrutation et à l'effet de rendre l'être présent à soi-même. Dans certains cas, notamment *One Second in Montreal*, *Up to the 8th floor*, *Bantar Gebang*, les *Screen Tests*, l'attente envahit à ce point notre expérience que l'esprit s'égare, délaisse l'œuvre, y revient, décroche à nouveau, plongeant ainsi le regardeur dans une durée syncopée, saisit momentanément par des pensées autres, quotidiennes, voire anodines.

ATTENTE ARRÊT MOUVEMENT STASE

L'attente se conjugue dans cette opposition mouvement/arrêt et mouvement/stase qui se joue dans les œuvres tout au long du parcours de l'exposition. Une opposition productive qui dans ses déclinaisons d'un extrême à l'autre scandent l'exposition et créent des réverbérations temporelles qui composent une durée matérielle. Les agissements du visiteur possèdent un rythme marqué. Le spectateur marche, s'arrête, s'asseoit, attend, reprend le parcours, est retenu, suspendu, repoussé par l'œuvre, se déplace pour sentir cette mouvance se réduire à un état de stase pour ensuite s'en libérer et passer ailleurs. De par son accentuation au sein des œuvres, ce rythme est en quelque sorte la trame de l'événement-durée et de son expérience. Pensons au jeu de la stase et du mouvement dans *Up to the 8th floor* et *Catarina* : le regardeur se trouvera simultanément aux prises avec les vitesses changeantes de l'image et la mobilité de son corps. Pensons à comment le plan fixe de *Bantar Gebang* accapare le regard et le corps du spectateur pour ensuite le libérer dès que le geste des rituels de l'existence quotidienne viennent animer la surface de l'image. Ce rythme crée, par ailleurs, un régime non seulement du regard dans le temps mais de l'écoute, non seulement de l'esprit mais du corps vivant.

OBSCURITÉ INCONGRUITÉ

Toutes ces activités autour de l'expérience de la durée se déploient dans cette étrange interaction de notre corps dans un espace plongé dans l'obscurité, illuminé par les seules projections et traversé par des bruits ambiants parfois difficilement identifiables (*Bantar Gebang, See You Later/Au revoir* [1990]), ou par des paroles interrompues, voire déformées par des manipulations quelconques (*Catarina, Side Seat Paintings Slides Sound Film*). Ce n'est pas tout à fait l'expérience cinéma tel que le décrit Barthes[1], car la liberté de se déplacer à sa guise est beaucoup plus grande même dans le cas des films de Snow et de Rijke/de Rooij qui sont présentés selon le mode cinéma avec un horaire de visionnement et un projectionniste. C'est en fait plutôt l'expérience du cinéma d'exposition, de l'exposition « boîte noire »[2]. Se promener, s'asseoir sur un banc ou au sol, s'appuyer au mur, fixer l'image, s'en approcher, balayer du regard les murs de l'espace, passer d'une salle à l'autre dans une semi-obscurité constante et artificielle crée un rapport d'incongruité avec l'espace et entre les visiteurs, une rupture importante entre le monde quotidien extérieur et l'exposition. Cette condition singulière de perception de l'espace et des images dans *Timelength* nous rend encore plus captif de l'œuvre, et de sa capacité de nous faire vivre une durée qui violente la temporalité.

FILM VIDÉO PROJECTION MONITEUR

Timelength veut amener le visiteur à vivre la durée dans son excès, comme étant indissociable de son procédé car cette incursion profondément matérielle dans le temps, appréhendée dans son épaisseur, est le produit de procédés et de modes de présentation bien distincts les uns des autres, à savoir la vidéo et le film ; la projection et la diffusion sur moniteur ; et la projection continue et selon un horaire de visionnement. Il était donc important de présenter en galerie des films et vidéos dans leur forme originale. Seuls les *Screen Tests* de Warhol tournés en 16mm et transférés sur DVD sont présentés sur moniteur. Aujourd'hui on fait de moins en moins la distinction entre film et vidéo : nombre d'artistes tournent en 35mm pour ensuite opérer un transfert sur le support numérique vidéo et certains cinéastes expérimentaux, dont Stan Brakhage, ont accepté d'effectuer le transfert de leur œuvre sur vidéo. S'il faut y prêter attention c'est que le film et la vidéo sont des processus et des modes de présentation différents qui produisent des images et une durée spécifiques à leur médium. *Timelength* a voulu rendre les divergences, décalages et effets de chacun présents.

FILM

Timelength propose trois films en 16mm de Michael Snow – *One Second in Montreal*, *Side Seat Slides Paintings Sound Film* et *See You Later/ Au revoir* – et un film en 35mm du duo hollandais Jeroen de Rijke et Willem de Rooij intitulé *Bantar Gebang*. Voyons comment ce dispositif de présentation constitue la durée différemment. Depuis 1994, Jeroen de Rijke et Willem de Rooij collaborent à la production de films conçus expressément pour une présentation en galerie ou muséale. Il vaut de noter que de Rijke/ de Rooij ne se décrivent pas comme cinéastes. À la différence de Michael Snow qui est lui connu comme cinéaste expérimental, et également comme peintre, sculpteur et musicien. Snow, par ailleurs, présente habituellement ses films en salle de projection.

Bantar Gebang est un film de 10 minutes tourné en 35mm ; ceux de Michael Snow, tournés en 16mm, sont d'une durée respective de 26, 20 et 18 minutes. Ces films sont présentés en galerie selon un horaire de visionnement et dans un espace qui leur est consacré. Le visiteur est donc tenu d'être présent à un certain moment s'il veut en faire l'expérience. Il devra prendre place et attendre que le projecteur soit mis en marche pour enfin visionner le film. Au bout de 10 ou 26 minutes l'image aura fondu au noir, le projectionniste éteindra le projecteur et le visiteur se lèvera et quittera la salle. Ce processus va à l'encontre du caractère plus indéterminé de l'expérience de l'image vidéo projetée en boucle. Dans ce cas, le visiteur est en effet libre de regarder l'œuvre quand il le désire. Il ne peut cependant pas régler le moment auquel son regard intervient dans le cycle de projection, d'où cette impression de ne pouvoir saisir la totalité de l'œuvre. Dans un visionnement déterminé à l'avance, comme c'est le cas pour les œuvres de Snow et de Rijke et de Rooij, le début et la fin de l'œuvre sont démarqués et l'expérience de la durée débute dans les moments d'expectative devant l'écran muet et vide qui précède le visionnement pour se terminer dans les moments après la disparition de l'image et l'arrêt du projecteur. En outre, le visionnement dans la position assise, la présence et le son du projecteur (bien qu'étouffé) – le rituel de la projection, sa théâtralité, pour ainsi dire – font partie intégrante de l'expérience de l'œuvre filmique projetée. Dans ces œuvres la durée opère donc selon trois modes interreliés : l'expectative dans la semi-obscurité de la salle avant le début de la projection, la durée dans le temps précis de la projection et la durée *dans* l'œuvre. Puisque les films de Snow et de Rijke et de Rooij sont des œuvres-durée – Snow allongeant et mettant à nue la durée, de Rijke/de Rooij la rendant implacable dans son envahissement progressif – la durée produite par le dispositif et le mode de présentation a pour effet de la mettre en abîme, de la situer encore plus hors du temps commun.

TRANSFERTS

Les *Screen Tests* d'Andy Warhol présentés sur moniteur dans *Timelength* sont à l'origine des films en 16mm de 4 minutes que le Andy Warhol Museum a transférés sur DVD. Ce sont les seules œuvres qui ne sont pas projetées dans l'exposition et dont le rapport est télévisuel pour le spectateur. Il y a donc déplacement dans le mode de présentation et de visionnement des films. Ce brouillage et cette contamination des procédés et des médias dans le cas des *Screen Tests* ont l'effet de nuancer l'expérience de la durée dans ces bouts de films que je qualifierais de plages intenses de durée. Warhol présentait souvent ses films dans son atelier, au Factory, pendant que d'autres activités se déroulaient. On les visionnait à sa guise et on n'était aucunement tenu au silence. La durée dans les *Screen Tests* est constituée d'une part, d'un sujet fixant son regard sur l'objectif (ou fixé par l'objectif) et d'autre part, du regard du spectateur devenant comme fixe à regarder cette tête emprisonnée par l'objectif et le cadrage de l'image. Mais dans l'atelier de Warhol l'expérience du regardeur devait être parasitée par l'activité ambiante. La durée *dans* l'œuvre pouvait, on peut le supposer, être entièrement évacuée. En galerie et sur moniteur, l'expérience a un tout autre caractère. De l'échelle plus intime du moniteur, il se crée une espèce d'union entre notre regard et celui du sujet (dévisagé) dévisageant (Ann Buchanan, Billy Name) l'objectif ou se mettant en scène (Walter Dainwood, Donyale Luna) devant celui-ci. Dans l'attente qui a l'effet de se densifier devant chaque *Test* il se dégage une durée exorbitée du cours des choses.

Par ailleurs, dans le contexte de *Timelength* et quarante ans après leur production, un adoucissement se produit, les *Test*s sont investis d'une dimension lyrique et parfois mélancolique qui était sûrement absente à l'époque En outre, tout cela contribue à la hiératisation de l'œuvre. Mais non sans une pointe d'ironie car les transformations sont multiples et ne sont pas sans faire écho à la nature même de l'œuvre warholienne qui jouait avec complaisance du mode reproductif et brouillait délibérément la notion d'authenticité. Dans ce rapport télévisuel et prosaïque avec l'œuvre et dans cette distanciation par rapport au mode de production, la durée n'est pas uniquement celle qui se dégage de cet exercice d'endurance plat – fixer l'objectif d'une caméra pendant quelques minutes – elle est aussi celle de la durée *dans le temps,* de la survie, qui transporte ces petits bouts de films ici et simultanément ailleurs.

VIDÉO

La durée dans les projections vidéo a sa propre spécificité. Dans cette exposition les projections sont continues, présentées sous forme de boucle. L'image est donc présente et accessible (sa dimension qui excède l'échelle humaine agit comme un plan d'attraction dans lequel le regardeur peut souvent s'y perdre) en tout temps et la durée fait partie d'un continuum dans l'espace. On pénètre dans son orbite on y reste suspendu pour un laps de temps, on le délaisse selon notre gré. L'attente chez Grandmaison, MacGregor et Robert, a uniquement lieu *dans* l'œuvre et puisque chacune de ces œuvres est constituée d'attente, la durée est d'autant plus matérielle. Si le dispositif de projection 16 ou 35mm produit de la durée par sa présence dans le champ de l'œuvre et fonctionne comme vecteur historique, ce n'est pas le cas pour le projecteur vidéo qui est plutôt un outil utilitaire. De plus, son usage relativement récent dans les expositions et son ubiquité dans les musées et galeries le privent de toute valeur symbolique. Dès que le visiteur pénètre dans l'espace il s'immisce dans l'image et, le cas échéant, dans le son qui, puisqu'ils sont présentés en continu, le préexistent et lui survivent. La présence de la durée peut donc plus facilement se confondre à l'espace, voire s'unir à elle, dans les œuvres de Grandmaison, MacGregor et Robert, et son expérience se vivre comme un étirement. Où il y aura changement de registre de la durée ce sera dans le temps soigneusement découpé, créé par la projection de films durant un temps fixe. Entre ces deux modes de présentation et de production d'images et de sons il en résulte finalement une durée dont la matérialité possède des pourtours fluctuants.

IMAGE SILENCE SON CORPS

Timelength nous confronte à des images qui, parfois sont multiples et successives (*Spin, Screen Tests, One Second in Montreal*), parfois s'inscrivent dans une séquence narrative (*One Second in Montreal, Side Seat, See You Later/Au revoir, Catarina*) et parfois sont une vue ou un plan unique, mais qui n'en subit pas moins de nombreuses et subtiles transformations dans sa séquence (*Bantar Gebang, Up to the 8th floor*). L'image exerce bien entendu sa fascination sur le visiteur et c'est sur ce mode que sont conçues bon nombre d'expositions qui s'articulent autour de l'image en projection. Or la présente exposition insiste non pas sur la seule « image » ou plus précisément sur le pouvoir unique de l'image-durée, mais sur l'image comme la part d'un ensemble produisant de la durée et qui comprend le son, le silence et le corps mais aussi, comme on l'a vu ci-haut, en tant qu'image rattachée à des dispositifs de présentation précis. Ainsi le silence accompagnant les œuvres de MacGregor et de Grandmaison, *One Second in Montreal* de Snow et les *Screen Tests* de Warhol qui est aussi bien une absence de son qu'une présence qui emplit l'espace, est une composante de la matérialisation de la durée dans l'image et de notre expérience de celle-ci comme excès et attente. Le son sous forme de bruits ambiants accentués dans *Bantar Gebang*, de la voix au récit interrompu dans *Catarina*, des distorsions que Snow a fait subir à la voix dans *Side Seat* et du martèlement des frappes de la machine à écrire dans *See You Later/ Au revoir* creuse à tout moment l'image-durée et scande le temps de l'attente.

Dans chaque cas le son ou le silence produit active en nous l'écoute et, partant, oblige un sens autre que celui de la vision à déterminer les paramètres de l'œuvre. Dans *Timelength* l'événement de la durée se vit dans un rapport qui fait s'imbriquer la vue, l'écoute et le corps en mouvement et au repos. *Timelength* est avant tout une mise en espace qui veut mettre de l'avant la complexité et les subtiles divergences et écarts dans les œuvres et dans leurs modes de présentation qui créent cette expérience d'un temps qui s'allonge et excède étrangement la temporalité.

NOTES

1. Roland Barthes, « En sortant du cinéma », *Le bruissement de la langue*, Essais critiques IV, Paris, Éd. du Seuil, coll. « Points Essais, p. 407-412.

2. Il existe un débat sur la question alimenté par une littérature sur le sujet. Voir « Quelques réflexions sur le « cinéma d'exposition » dans ce catalogue.

FILMIC TIME IN INSTALLATION

Stefan Jovanovič

> The cinema was born – and this is no small matter – as a machine to produce images, views that were continuous, unbroken, lengthy. From the outset filmic time was given as a time to which one submits and simultaneously as an acknowledged, identified time: unable to escape the time of projection, we nevertheless accept this time, recognize it as our own, and experience it as such. This is the meaning of Jean-Louis Schefer's famous description of the cinema as "the only experience in which time is given to me as a perception."
>
> Jacques Aumont, "The Variable Eye, or the Mobilization of the Gaze" [1]

Visual artists have increasingly taken on the role of filmmaker, and, within this movement, it is more than simply the cinema's materials, techniques and repertoire that have been displaced into the museum and the gallery; most significantly, it is the cinema's modes of reception. We experience countless moving images within the spaces of contemporary art, many of which reproduce and critique (or at least problematize) the aesthetic and experiential qualities of cinema. The projected film or video installation is the most familiar manifestation of this phenomenon. I would like to introduce a reading of some of the kinds of cinema we encounter within exhibition spaces from the point of view of *duration*, which is a necessary condition of cinematic representation. Film implies duration – conceptually as well as materially – and we must thus negotiate a relationship to *filmic time* each time we experience the moving-image projection in a visual arts environment. In outlining some of the ideas formulated in several recent studies addressing the origins of cinema and aspects of visual culture within late modernity, I shall suggest that contemporary film and video installations summon up identifiable modes of filmic duration in their formal and figurative strategies, in what may thereby amount to a concurring critical practice. Specifically, I would claim that these artworks' construction of meaning within filmic time enact, in a kind of interdiscursive exchange with film history and theory, a *double movement* – a rethinking or rewriting of cinema's past in light of a 'post-cinematic condition' theorized in the present moment. Or, in other words, I'd like to think about the ways in which contemporary art, by recourse to duration and the luminous screen, seems to have undertaken an obsessive *revisiting* of cinema. In this context, 'to revisit' might be understood to connote both forestalling and superseding the cinema's oft-anticipated demise, which surely has been one of the most influential tropes within this genre of art practice.[2] Duration therefore also implies a forestalling of the end to cinema, and, in light of the ongoing postulations of the cinema's death – recurrent and often misleading and hyperbolic – these critical practices would seem to have undertaken a kind of rewriting of its historical beginnings.[3]

A key concern in contemporary discussions of modern visual culture and the shaping of experience in late modernity has been the role of the cinema and its changing aesthetic and phenomenological modalities within the 'subjectivization' of the spectator. Accordingly, the theorization of the social and psychic conditions of film reception in many recent studies will have either revised or dispensed with such vague and mediocre notions as 'the cinematic effect' and a fixed 'apparatus' of the enclosed and darkened theatre, "where the spectator – captive and immobilized in his armchair – is also captured by the film, fastened to the screen in a play of seduction and identification," as Jacques Aumont has written.[4] In dealing with broader socio-historical aspects of technique, models of vision, and the origins of modern visual culture in the nineteenth and early twentieth centuries, Aumont and a number of other scholars[5] have argued that the relationship between the viewer and the spectacle of cinema – a dynamic historical configuration specific to late modernity – generates not *one* effect, but many. And the inexorable changes to film's contexts of reception throughout its history would suggest that one could not rely on any enduring material configuration to provide the ground for some transhistorical 'apparatus' model of cinematic reception. "What is called 'the cinema' has in fact entailed throughout its history many different modes in the material presentation of the film to a spectator," Aumont notes, citing such examples as early cinema's 'nickelodeon' (a mostly standing-room audience), the drive-in and non-Western contexts of film spectatorship.[6] The rethinking of materialist socio-historical and phenomenological accounts of the cinema by referencing their concepts to this wider set of critical concerns and theoretical models has thus sought to resituate the origin of cinema – and to understand its heterogeneous and ever-changing conditions of reception – within a fundamental historical and cultural rupture in models of vision, attention and temporality in Western modernity.[7] For Aumont, the preconditions for cinematic reception were to be found amid a longer and more profound epistemic shift in models of vision. The model of the 'disembodied' gaze in which the camera obscura stood as the metaphor for vision during the classical age, Aumont has argued, gives way to a 'variable eye,' a new embodied or 'corporeal' and mobilized gaze typical of the spectator's relationship to cinema. This variable eye and modern visual culture echo other developments in the nineteenth century, including new modes in painting and the advent of rail travel and photography. This variable eye represents, for Aumont, "the configuration of modernity par excellence."[8]

What is essential to the cinema therefore, (if we accept the theoretical terms of Aumont's model), lies neither with the film medium, nor with the various institutions of cinema. Rather, it is located within this relationship of self-divestiture negotiated between viewer and spectacle within filmic duration. As Jean-Louis Schefer declares in the introductory quote above, the cinema offers its spectator *time as a perception*. If the cinema comprises any enduring feature, it may be only film's concrete and irreversible duration in real time that we submit to, of necessity, as spectators. This relationship is negotiated within the varying conditions of viewing a luminous image that occupies a two-dimensional surface, but is not reducible to any single context or set-up. Nor does the experience of temporal continuity require any essential correspondence of this mediated image to any lived spatial or temporal reality, although the cinema's epistemological claims are a function of the moving image's ability to mediate real space-times with an unsurpassed degree of verisimilitude. To submit to the time of the cinema is to relinquish the possibility of control over the moving image, in contrast to the experiences of temporal interactivity afforded by "video games and other simulations," or what Aumont defines as "today's 'new images.'"[9] In such images, as Aumont understands them, "time is 'interactively' masterable and almost entirely manipulable."[10] We might thereby claim that insofar as a moving image installation unfolds in concrete duration and defies any kind of temporal manipulation or mastery on the viewer's part, such an artwork reiterates the most irreducibly cinematic strategy – the presentation of filmic duration. In the context of the visual art space, such a viewer-spectacle configuration, I would posit, probably remains much closer to the viewer-object paradigm of modern art's reception[11] than the user-object relationship expressed through such cultural forms and techniques as video games, new media and the Internet. It may be observed that a good many of the multimedia works one encounters in today's visual arts environments lay claim to the kind of 'post-cinematic' discourse Aumont might associate with the advent of a postmodern 'demobilization' of vision, as typified by the user's relationship to virtual reality and cyberspace. And, in considering the proliferation of these new images as marking the coextensive twilight of the modern viewer-spectacle paradigm represented by the variable eye, the author thereby concludes that the cinema too, must inevitably reach its end: "the camera has now become a cold eye, completely void of all reference to the human that transported the cinema to its apogee. The variable eye, too, has entered the era of postmodernity."[12]

Aumont's study offers a persuasive model for understanding the central place of theories of modernity and modern visual culture within considerations of filmic time. I would like to pursue this line of inquiry by introducing into this model some of the ideas put forth by Mary Ann Doane's recent book, *The Emergence of Cinematic Time*.[13] Doane's detailed study of the origin of cinematic time and of the cinema's capacity to represent duration situates this development within the changed models of temporality in late modernity, specifically the increasing standardization and management of time effected by modern techniques and capitalist production. Discussing the thorny issue of film's indexical relation to time in early cinema, the author introduces the concept of 'the event' as the 'unassimilable' contingency implicit in the recording of time by the camera. For Doane, the 'event' implies a twofold notion within this context: that of temporal continuity and structure, but also of transience, chance and unpredictability. Doane writes:

> Insofar as the cinema presented itself as the indexical record of time, it allied itself with the event and the unfolding of events as aleatory, stochastic, contingent. It was capable of trapping events in all their unpredictability and pure factualness. However, the fact of its own finitude – the limits imposed by both the frame and the length of the reel – resulted in the necessity of conceiving the event simultaneously in terms of structure as a unit of time, as not simply a happening but a significant happening that nevertheless remained tinged by the contingent, by the unassimilable. This curious merger of contingency and structure lends specificity to the early formations of cinematic temporality.[14]

I want to consider Doane's remarks in relation to the body of films produced by Andy Warhol, probably the key figure in avant-garde film's connection to the contemporary use of the moving image in the visual arts. Warhol's film corpus prefigures in many respects the double movement that, I have suggested, marks the relationship between early cinematic notions of temporality and the re-engagement with these models by contemporary film and videomakers. In contrast to the early avant-gardes' use of montage for its modern 'shock-effect,' Warhol's principal innovation in his early films was to *eliminate* editing, splicing together only the end of one film reel to the beginning of the next. Such a practice underscores what I would declare to be a critical aspect of Warhol's work in film: a continual double reflection on early cinematic time and the unstable beginnings of film culture vis-à-vis the upheavals within the domain of the moving image taking place in the 1960s. Writing in 1964, Jonas Mekas declared that "Andy Warhol is taking cinema back to its origins, to the days of Lumière, for a rejuvenation and a cleansing."[15] And indeed, the trajectory of Warhol's film work, as Hoberman has noted, appears to emulate the historical development of the cinema itself. It evolves from silent black-and-white, single-reel films such as *Kiss* (1963), to the gradual incorporation of sound, scenarios, and even the short-lived use of two and three screen set-ups (echoing the groundbreaking work of the silent film pioneer Abel Gance) in films such as *Chelsea Girls* (1966). Warhol's films would appear to follow this model through to the use of colour, editing, widescreen, and finally, the production of feature films (1974's *Frankenstein* even being presented in 3D).[16] The extremely long, silent, fixed-frame films of Warhol's early period provide perhaps the best example of how the artist invokes the paradoxes of early cinematic time – the notion of temporal continuity achieved through a succession of fixed images – as a means to critique the various rhetorics of cinematic 'realism' in postwar European modernism, documentary and ethnographic film. In examining the influence of Warhol's approach toward filmic time on the work of Chantal Ackerman, Ivone Margulies writes: "Warhol undermines observational and direct cinema by hyperbolizing to the point of caricature the very basis of their existence: the notion of non-interference."[17] Margulies further asserts that, " Warhol's extended renditions of cliché images create a different register through which to read neorealism's narrativized phenomenology of the quotidian."[18] Warhol challenges the cinema's epistemological and narrative foundations by undermining the cinematic notions of event and of contingency, presenting instead a fixed-frame image of pure sameness, thereby amplifying the formal and figurative effects of cinematic duration.

Mainstream cinema shows a strong disinclination to what we call 'dead time,' any length of time in a film that does not contribute to advancing the film's narrative. In Warhol's longer films, such as *Sleep* and *Empire,* the artist presents us with nothing but dead time, a subtle filmic entropy brought nearly to the point of stasis by its fixity of framing and un-dynamic composition (not to mention being projected at 16 frames per second instead of 24). For, as Doane might argue, dead time undermines the illusionistic distraction from lived time that is the basic lure of cinema to the modern spectator. Dead time tends to create awareness on the part of the spectator of lived time outside the diegesis and the frame of the film, thereby, in effect, negating (or at least mitigating) the seduction of cinema. The dead time of these films thus creates a dual register of temporal experience. For even as the viewer inspects the surface of Warhol's moving image for evidence of the film's 'event-ness' in such contingencies as scratches and jumps, the graininess of the film and so on, he or she becomes aware of the lived time outside of the frame of the film, within which nothing seems to happen. Such films, as Margulies has argued, simultaneously emphasize both the film's materiality and a very literal form of referentiality.[19]

Warhol's double reflection on early cinematic time also references the unstable norms and conventions of early cinema in bringing the reception of his films closer to the idea of a museum or gallery viewing protocol. Unlike other avant-garde films of the 1960s, including the 'structural' film movement within which these films are often inscribed, the artist himself never watched them in their entirety and preferred his viewers likewise to come and go as they pleased. Thus, in terms of the external duration of the time of viewing, such a format of presentation sets Warhol's work in sharp contrast to the structural filmmaker's reliance on the more rigid and immobile viewing protocol of the darkened cinema. Specifically, the mode of reception within which one might experience Warhol's *Sleep* would set it in contrast phenomenologically, as well as conceptually, with a film such as Michael Snow's *La Région Centrale* (1971), which implicitly demands that the viewer take in its entire three hours' duration, given that the latter work is largely premised on the increasingly dizzying, hallucinatory and visceral effect on its *captive* audience.

Snow's films, though addressed to an immobile spectator in the cinema, are equally exemplary of the kinds of radicalized film practice being done throughout the 1960s and early 1970s, although the artist takes a somewhat different approach in formulating the terms of his critique vis-à-vis cinematic illusionism and the modalities of filmic duration. Snow's 1990 offering, the 18-minute *See You Later/Au revoir* stages the most banal non-event (a man leaving an office) and slows it down almost to the point of immobility through the use of high speed photography to film this action at a rate of thousands of frames per second. The effect of this extreme distension of a roughly 30-second action introduces an extraordinarily sculptural and almost suspenseful quality into a banal action. In re-presenting the temporal continuity of so fleeting and arbitrary a narrative moment – one which conventionally would be subsumed under the seamless formal system of continuity-cutting in a mainstream film – in such concrete and palpable terms of filmic duration, Snow gives new meaning to the kind of surgical penetration that Walter Benjamin ascribed to the work of the cinema's cameraman with respect to the subject being recorded.[20] *See You Later/Au revoir* pushes to extremes this metaphorical penetration, enacting an almost phantasmic spectacle out of a brief and otherwise unremarkable action.

Contemporary artists have devised a diversity of strategies that would appear to carry forward the critical aims of avant-garde cinema, reproducing and challenging the different historical conditions of cinema's viewer-spectacle relationship. Underpinning this orientation, as I have already discussed, has been a range of scholarly discourse correlating the changing norms and conventions of contemporary film and media reception with the unstable permutations of early modern visual culture, within which the cinema was but one – albeit particularly compelling – technological and cultural form.[21] As Leo Charney and Vanessa R. Schwartz have written: "Cinema constituted only one element in an array of new modes of technology, representation, spectacle, distraction, consumerism, ephemerality, mobility, and entertainment – and at many points neither the most compelling nor the most promising one."[22] The advent of new historicism, as a method of looking into early cinema in modern culture, thereby reflects a more general interest in different modes of consciousness and formulations of subjectivity, within which the cinema and forms of cinematic duration are inscribed. Such a hypothesis might be underscored in part by the prevalence within contemporary film and video of figures, formal structures, and techniques of staging duration, that invoke early or primitive cinema, 1960s and 1970s avant-garde film, and European modernist narrative as the most frequent point of reference. Hence, Warhol's critical place in linking together avant-garde film practices of the 1960s with the gallery-based cinema of contemporary art. Unlike many of his contemporaries who moved from painting into sculpture in the early 1960s, Warhol shifted his attention to film. Warhol's concern with the literality created by his use of extreme duration and dead time offers a viewing experience of the cinema that, in Margulies's view, is hyperrealist in its literality.

The consequences for cinema of Warhol's hyperrealist cinema, the author concludes, entails a problematization, or perhaps even a throwing into question, of the epistemology that underpins literal and figurative modes of cinematic representation in general. In a media environment increasingly saturated with mass entertainment that conflates reality and representation, and whose use of duration mirrors the unstable generic categories of early cinema, contemporary art's recourse to literal time can be regarded as an attempt to undermine the illusory seduction of these novel cultural forums. Such strategies are, at their most basic, the staging of cinematic duration with no need of recourse to the materials, techniques and repertoire of cinema. For example, Douglas Gordon's *Twenty-Four Hour Psycho* (1993) puts filmic duration in a sort of suspended animation, using (paradoxically enough) a VCR and VHS copy of Hitchcock's *Psycho*. Such a work highlights the arbitrariness of cinema's material features and contexts of reception in the formulation of staging duration.

Invoking these different conceptions of cinematic time, contemporary art re-engages (without simply reiterating) the avant-garde's critique of cinematic illusionism in presenting, to a viewer who is increasingly accustomed to manipulating moving images, a configuration that deliberately denies this possibility and, rather, exaggerates and intensifies the unmasterable quality of cinematic time. This occurs through permutations of duration realized through forms such as multiple screens or channels, the temporal form of the loop, and fixed screening time for gallery installations. In the latter instance, for example, Dutch film artists de Rijke/de Rooij frequently present their films in the gallery at fixed screening times, preferring viewers to watch each film in its entirety. In their installation entitled *Bantar Gebang* (2000), duration takes the form of a kind of phenomenological wavering between fixity and movement of the photographic image; this encounter – created within the context of a gallery experience that explicitly evokes the conventions of the traditional cinema – seems to prompt, through such a viewing protocol, a specifically immersive form of contemplation.

My aim herein has not been simply to reiterate the oft-repeated argument that 1960s avant-garde cinema atavistically refers to early cinema in its formal and aesthetic modalities, and that contemporary film and video practices carry forward this same project. Rather, I have aimed to highlight some of the possible theoretical points of reference, by recourse to which contemporary works re-engage earlier models of cinematic reception in their use of duration. If, as film theorists have suggested, these mutable qualities of duration compel us to reconsider the conceptual basis of cinematic forms of visual rhetoric, or even the very epistemology of the cinematic image, then the influx of filmic practices into the museum perhaps points to the exhaustedness of other venues for critical exchange between viewer and cinematic image. That public space and television, as possible sites of diffusion, are too monopolized by advertising to accommodate any kind of critical reflection, would seem to imply that the museum may remain the only space within which these phenomenological and aesthetic modalities of the moving image may be critiqued. This perhaps may be the horizon where the *cinéma d'exposition* may recuperate a kind of critical potential.

NOTES

1. Jacques Aumont, "The Variable Eye, or the Mobilization of the Gaze," trans. Charles O'Brien and Sally Shafto, in Dudley Andrew, ed. *The image in dispute: art and cinema in the age of photography* (Austin: University of Texas Press, 1997) p. 245. This essay comprises the second chapter of Aumont's book *L'Oeil interminable : cinéma et peinture* (Paris: Séguier, 1989). [*L'Oeil interminable*, p. 58.]

2. See for instance Emmanuel Hermange, « Pour nous le cinéma est mort : Notes sur quelques stratégies cinéphiles de l'art. » *Parachute* no. 103 (07-08-09/2001) pp. 12-25.

3. We might compare the cinema's double-movement to that of photography. It has for some time now been suggested that advances in digital imaging and the proliferation of pictures thereby generated are foreshadowing a 'post-photographic' future: that no image will be able to make a claim to 'visual truth' by virtue of its indexical relation to a pre-existing 'reality'. Conversely, the re-writing of photography's emergence has challenged the notion of 'indexicality' as intrinsic to formations of a photographic epistemology during its early history. See especially, William J. Mitchell, *The Reconfigured Eye: Visual Truth in the Post-Photographic Era* (Cambridge, Mass. and London: MIT Press, 1992) and Geoffrey Batchen, *Burning With Desire: The Conception of Photography* (Cambridge, Mass. and London: MIT Press, 1997).

4. Aumont, *op.cit.* p. 241 [« Nous n'imaginons plus guère d'autre modèle théorique du spectateur que celui où, captif, immobilisé dans son fauteil, il est aussi « captivé » par le film, rivé à l'écran par le jeu de la séduction et de l'identification. » *L'Oeil interminable,* p. 52.]

5. See especially the collection *Early Cinema: Space, Frame, Narrative*, edited by Thomas Elsaesser (London: BFI, 1990).

6. Aumont, *op.cit.* p. 241. [« Ce qu'on appelle « le » cinéma a connu, en fait, et à toutes les époques, bien de modes différents de présentation matérielle du film au spectateur. » *L'Oeil interminable,* p. 52.]

7. See Jonathan Crary, *Suspensions of Perception: Attention, Spectacle and Modern Culture* (Cambridge, Mass. and London: MIT Press, 1999).

8. Aumont, *op.cit.* p. 247. [« la configuration moderne par excellence. » *L'Oeil interminable,* p. 60.]

9. Aumont, *op.cit.* p. 256, n. 28. [« les jeux vidéo et autres simulations. » *L'Oeil interminable*, p. 72.]

10. *Ibid.* [« nul moyen pour le spectateur d'accélérer ni de ralentir le film, à la différence, radicale, des « nouvelles images », dont le temps est « interactivement » maîtrisable, presque déformable. » Jacques Aumont, *L'Oeil interminable*, p. 58.]

11. For a discussion of the relationship between modern art and experimental film of the 1960s and 70s from the point of view of time and theatricality, see Ivone Margulies, *Nothing Happens: Chantal Ackerman's Hyperrealist Everyday* (Durham, NC and London: Duke University Press, 1996), Ch. 2: "Toward a Corporeal Cinema," pp. 42-64.

12. Aumont, *op.cit.* p. 249. [« la caméra devient un œil froid, parfaitement vidé de la référence à l'humain que charriait, à son apogée encore, le cinéma. Tout simplement, l'œil variable est entré, lui aussi, dans le postmoderne. » *L'Oeil interminable*, p. 63.]

13. Mary Ann Doane, *The Emergence of Cinematic Time: Modernity, Contingency, the Archive* (Cambridge, Mass. and London: Harvard University Press, 2002)

14. *Ibid.*, p. 140-141.

15. Quoted in Jim Hoberman, "After Avant-Garde Film," in Brian Wallis, ed. *Art After Modernism: Rethinking Representation* (New York: New Museum of Contemporary Art; Boston : D.R. Godine, 1984) p. 63.

16. *Ibid.*

17. Ivone Margulies, *Nothing Happens,* p. 37.

18. *Ibid.*, p. 38.

19. *Ibid.*

20. Walter Benjamin, "The Work of Art in the Age of Mechanical Reproduction," in *Illuminations*, ed. Hannah Arendt, trans. Harry Zohn (New York, Schocken, 1969), p. 233.

21. See Leo Charney and Vanessa R. Schwartz, eds. *Cinema and the Invention of Modern Life* (Berkeley: University of California Press, 1995); Anne Friedberg, *Window Shopping: Cinema and the Postmodern* (Berkeley and Los Angeles: University of California Press, 1993).

22. Leo Charney and Vanessa R. Schwartz, "Introduction," *Cinema and the Invention of Modern Life*, p. 1.

LE TEMPS FILMIQUE DANS L'INSTALLATION

Stefan Jovanovič

> Le cinéma est né, c'est loin d'être indifférent, comme machine à produire des images – des *vues* – continues, non morcelées, longues. D'emblée le temps filmique a été donné comme un temps à la fois subi [...] et reconnu, identifié : nous ne pouvons échapper au temps qui s'écoule dans la projection, et cependant, ce-pendant nous y adhérons, le reconnaissons comme notre propre temps, le vivons comme tel. (C'est le sens dans la fameuse formule de Jean-Louis Chéfer [*sic*] sur le cinéma, «*la seule expérience dans laquelle le temps m'est donné comme une perception* »).
>
> Jacques Aumont, « L'Œil variable, ou la mobilisation du regard » [1]

De plus en plus, les artistes visuels assument le rôle de cinéaste, déplaçant dans les musées et les galeries d'art non seulement le matériel, la technique et le répertoire du cinéma, mais surtout les modes de sa réception. Les espaces d'art contemporain foisonnent d'images en mouvement, dont bon nombre reproduisent et critiquent (ou du moins questionnent) les qualités esthétiques et expériencielles du cinéma. La projection filmique et l'installation vidéo constituent les manifestations les plus courantes de ce phénomène. J'aimerais proposer une lecture de certains types de cinéma intégrés aux aires d'exposition du point de vue de la « durée », qui est une condition essentielle à la représentation filmique. Qui dit film dit durée, tant conceptuelle que matérielle. Il nous faut donc négocier un rapport au *temps filmique* à toutes les fois que nous assistons à une projection d'images en mouvement en milieu d'arts visuels. Partant de certaines idées énoncées dans plusieurs études récentes sur les origines du cinéma et les aspects de la culture visuelle dans la modernité tardive, j'entends suggérer que les installations filmiques et vidéographiques contemporaines mettent à contribution des modes connus du temps filmique dans leurs stratégies formelles et figuratives, représentant de ce fait une pratique critique concomitante. Plus particulièrement, j'avancerais que la construction de sens de ces œuvres d'art à l'intérieur du temps filmique agit, dans une sorte d'échange discursif entre l'histoire et la théorie du cinéma, comme un *double mouvement* – une réinterprétation ou une relecture du passé du cinéma à la lumière de la notion de « pré-cinéma » actuellement mise en théorie. Autrement dit, j'aimerais examiner les façons par lesquelles l'art contemporain, en recourant à la durée et à l'écran lumineux, semble avoir entrepris une réinterprétation obsessionnelle du cinéma. Ici, « réinterpréter » peut suggérer à la fois l'anticipation et le remplacement de la fin maintes fois annoncée du cinéma, qui s'est avérée un des tropes les plus usités de cette pratique artistique[2]. La durée sous-entend donc également une anticipation de la fin du cinéma et à la lumière des postulats actuels sur la mort du cinéma – récurrents et souvents trompeurs et hyperboliques – ces pratiques critiques semblent avoir entrepris une certaine réinterprétation de ses débuts historiques[3].

Le rôle du cinéma et l'évolution de ses modalités esthétiques et phénoménologiques gouvernant le concept de spectateur reconnu comme « sujet regardant» est au cœur des débats actuels sur la culture visuelle moderne et la définition de l'expérience dans la modernité tardive. Par conséquent, les théories sur les conditions sociales et psychiques de la réception filmique formulées dans de nombreuses études récentes tendent soit à repenser soit à éliminer des notions aussi vagues et médiocres que celles de l'« effet cinéma » et du « dispositif » de la salle de cinéma plongée dans la pénombre où, selon Jacques Aumont, le « [..] spectateur [...] captif, immobilisé dans son fauteuil, [...] est aussi « captivé » par le film, rivé à l'écran par le jeu de la séduction et de l'identification »[4]. Abordant les aspects socio-historiques plus larges de la technique, des modèles de vision et des origines de la culture visuelle moderne au dix-neuvième siècle et au début du vingtième siècle, Aumont et plusieurs autres théoriciens[5] soutiennent que le rapport entre le spectateur et le spectacle du cinéma – une configuration historique dynamique propre à la modernité tardive – engendre non pas *un* effet, mais plusieurs. Les changements draconiens des contextes de la réception à travers l'histoire du cinéma suggèrent qu'on ne saurait se fier à une configuration matérielle durable pour l'élaboration d'un modèle transhistorique de réception filmique. « Ce qu'on appelle « le » cinéma a connu en fait, et à toutes les époques, bien des modes différents de présentation matérielle du film au spectateur[6] », fait valoir Aumont, citant en exemple le « nickolodeon » (où seuls les spectateurs des premiers rangs étaient assis), le ciné-parc et le cinéma non-occidental. Toute réinterprétation des constats matérialistes socio-historiques et phénoménologiques par une mise en rapport de leurs concepts à cet ensemble élargi de préoccupations critiques et modèles théoriques vise à resituer les débuts du cinéma (et à en examiner les conditions de réception hétérogènes et toujours changeantes) à l'intérieur d'une rupture historique et culturelle fondamentale des modèles de vision, d'attention et de temporalité dans la modernité occidentale[7]. Pour Aumont les conditions préalables de la réception filmique se trouvaient parmi une rupture épistémique plus longue et plus profonde des modèles de vision. Selon lui, le modèle du regard « désincarné » dans lequel la chambre noire représentait la métaphore de la vision à l'âge classique cède à un « œil variable », un nouveau regard incarné ou corporel et mobilisé typique du rapport entre le spectateur et le cinéma. Cet œil variable et cette culture visuelle moderne font écho aux autres développements du dix-neuvième siècle, y compris les nouveaux modes de peinture et l'avènement du chemin de fer et de la photographie. Pour Aumont, l'œil variable représente « la configuration moderne par excellence[8] ».

Par conséquent, ce qui est essentiel au cinéma – si nous acceptons les principes du modèle d'Aumont – ne participe ni du médium filmique, ni des diverses institutions du cinéma. Il réside plutôt au cœur du rapport d'abandon négocié entre le spectateur et le spectacle à l'intérieur du temps filmique. Pour reprendre les mots de Jean-Louis Schefer cité plus haut, le cinéma offre au spectateur le *temps comme perception*. Si le cinéma comprend une caractéristique durable, elle se résume peut-être à la durée concrète et irréversible du film en temps réel à laquelle le spectateur est obligatoirement assujetti. Ce rapport est négocié à l'intérieur des conditions variables du visionnement d'une image lumineuse qui occupe une surface bidimensionnelle, mais qui ne peut être limitée à un contexte ou une mise en scène en particulier. Non plus que l'expérience de la continuité temporelle n'exige que cette image médiatisée corresponde à une réalité spatiale ou temporelle vécue. Cela dit, les revendications épistémologiques du cinéma dépendent de la capacité de l'image animée de médiatiser des espaces-temps réels d'une vraisemblance inégalée. Se soumettre au temps filmique c'est renoncer à la possiblité de contrôler l'image animée, à la différence des expériences d'interactivité temporelle que procurent « les jeux vidéos et autres simulations[9] » qu'Aumont qualifie de « nouvelles images dont le temps est « interactivement » maîtrisable, presque déformable[10] ». De ce fait, nous pourrions affirmer que dans la mesure où une installation à image animée se déploie dans une durée concrète et défie toute déformation ou maîtrise temporelle de la part du spectateur, elle confirme la stratégie filmique la plus irréductible, soit la présentation du temps filmique. Je poserais comme postulat que dans le contexte de l'espace d'art visuel, cette configuration spectateur-spectacle se rapproche probablement davantage du paradigme spectateur-objet de la réception de l'art moderne[11] que du rapport usager-objet exprimé sous diverses formes et techniques culturelles – jeux vidéo, nouveaux médias et Internet. Il vaut de souligner que bon nombre des œuvres multimédias actuelles participent du discours « post-cinéma » qu'Aumont associerait à l'avènement d'une « démobilisation » post-moderne de la vision, parfaitment illustrée par le rapport entre l'usager et la réalité virtuelle et le cyberespace[12]. L'auteur, pour qui la prolifération de ces nouvelles images marque le crépuscule du paradigme spectateur-spectacle moderne représenté par l'œil variable, conclut que le cinéma tire inévitablement à sa fin : « la caméra devient un œil froid, parfaitement vidé de la référence à l'humain que charriait, à son apogée encore, le cinéma. Tout simplement, l'œil variable est entré, lui aussi, dans le post-moderne[12]. »

Aumont propose un modèle convaincant pour comprendre la place essentielle qu'occupent les théories de la modernité et de la culture visuelle moderne dans le cadre des préoccupations du temps filmique. J'aimerais poursuivre cette piste d'enquête en intégrant à ce modèle certaines des idées mises de l'avant dans l'ouvrage récent de Mary Ann Doane intitulé *The Emergence of Cinematic Time*[13]. L'étude détaillée de l'auteur sur l'origine du temps filmique et la capacité du cinéma à représenter le temps situe ce développement à l'intérieur des nouveaux modèles de la temporalité de la modernité tardive, en particulier la normalisation et la gestion du temps effectuées par les techniques modernes et la production capitaliste. Abordant la question épineuse de la relation indexicale entre le film et le temps aux débuts du cinéma, Doane introduit la notion de « l'événement » en tant que l'éventualité « non-assimilable » implicite dans l'enregistrement du temps par la caméra. Pour Doane, l'événement sous-entend une double notion à l'intérieur de ce contexte : celle de la continuité et de la structure temporelle, et celle de l'éphémère, du hasard et de l'imprévu. Doane écrit :

> Dans la mesure où le cinéma se présentait comme l'enregistrement indexical du temps, il s'assimilait à l'événement et au déroulement des événements comme aléatoire, stochastique, imprévu. Il était capable de figer les événements dans tout ce qu'ils avaient d'imprévisible et de factuel. Cependant, le fait de sa propre finitude – les limites imposées à la fois par le cadrage et la longueur de la bobine – a entraîné la nécessité de concevoir l'événement simultanément en fonction de la structure comme unité temporelle et non seulement comme un happening, mais un happening important qui portait toujours l'empreinte de l'imprévu, du non-assimilable. Cette fusion insolite de l'imprévu

et de la structure confère une certaine spécificité aux premières manifestations de la temporalité filmique.[14]

Je vais examiner les propos de Doane à la lumière du corpus filmique d'Andy Warhol, qui a joué un rôle clé d'intermédiaire dans le rapport entre le cinéma d'avant-garde et l'intégration de l'image animée dans les arts visuels. Les films de Warhol préfigurent à de nombreux égards le double mouvement qui, tel que j'ai avancé ci-haut, marque le rapport entre les premières notions filmiques de la temporalité et la réactualisation de ces modèles par des cinéastes et vidéastes contemporains. À la différence des pionniers de l'avant-garde qui recouraient au montage pour son effet choc, à ses débuts Warhol se distingue en *éliminant* le montage, préférant coller les bobines bout à bout. Cette pratique met en valeur ce qui est à mon avis un aspect critique du travail filmique de Warhol : une double réflexion continue sur les débuts du temps filmique et sur les débuts incertains de la culture filmique par rapport aux bouleversements dans le domaine de l'image animée durant les années 60. En 1964, Jonas Mekas écrivait « Andy Warhol ramène le cinéma à ses origines, à l'époque des frères Lumière, il lui fait subir une cure de rajeunissement et une purification[15]. » Effectivement, la trajectoire de l'œuvre filmique de Warhol, comme l'a noté J. Hoberman, semble imiter le développement historique du cinéma même – depuis les films muets noir et blanc à bobine unique comme *Kiss* (1963) jusqu'à l'intégration progressive d'éléments sonores et de scénarios, voire même l'utilisation brève de deux ou trois écrans (à la manière des innovations du pionnier du cinéma muet Abel Gance) dans des films tels que *Chelsea Girls* (1966). Les films de Warhol semblent suivre ce modèle par leur utilisation de la couleur, du montage, de l'écran large et finalement de la production de longs métrages (*Frankenstein* (1974) fut même présenté en 3D)[16]. Les films muets interminables à cadre fixe des débuts de Warhol offrent peut-être le meilleur exemple de la façon dont l'artiste évoque les paradoxes des débuts du temps filmique – la notion de continuité temporelle réalisée à travers une succession de plans fixes – pour critiquer les discours du réalisme filmique du modernisme, du documentaire et du cinéma ethnographique de l'Europe de l'après-guerre. Dans son examen de l'influence de l'approche de Warhol à l'égard du temps filmique sur le travail de Chantal Ackerman, Ivone Margulies écrit : « Warhol déstabilise le cinéma direct et le cinéma d'observation en exagérant jusqu'à la caricature la base même de leur existence : la notion de non-interférence[17]. » Elle ajoute « chez Warhol l'usage exhaustif de clichés crée un registre différent pour la lecture du récit phénoménologique néoréaliste du quotidien[18]. »

Warhol conteste les bases épistémologiques et narratologiques du cinéma en remettant en question les notions filmiques de l'événement et de l'imprévu, présentant plutôt une image fixe de la plus pure uniformité, amplifiant ainsi les effets formels et figuratifs du temps filmique.

Le cinéma traditionnel est peu enclin à faire usage de que nous appelons le « temps mort » : toute période de temps qui ne contribue pas au déroulement du récit filmique. Les films les plus longs de Warhol, tels que *Sleep* et *Empire*, ne représentent rien d'autre que du temps mort, une entropie filmique discrète menée au point de quasi-stase par la fixité du cadre et le non dynamisme de la composition (sans parler du fait qu'il est projeté à 16 plans par seconde plutôt que 24). Comme Doane pourrait l'avancer, le temps mort amoindrit la distraction illusoire du temps réel qui constitue le principal attrait du cinéma pour le spectateur. Le temps mort sensibilise le spectateur au temps réel à l'extérieur de la diégèse et du récit du film et ce faisant annule (ou au moins atténue) la séduction du cinéma. Les temps morts des films de Warhol créent donc un double registre de l'expérience temporelle. Car au moment même où le spectateur examine la surface de l'image animée pour des traces de « l'événementialité » du film – égratignures, sauts, grain de la pellicule, etc., – il a conscience du temps réel à l'extérieur du cadre du film où il semble ne rien se passer. Selon Margulies, ces films insistent simultanément sur la matérialité du film et sur une forme très littérale de la référentialité[19].

La double réflexion de Warhol sur les débuts du temps filmique fait également référence aux normes et conventions changeantes des débuts du cinéma en rattachant la réception de ses films au protocole de visionnement d'un musée ou d'une galerie d'art. À la différence des autres films d'avant-garde des années 60, y compris le cinéma structurel auquel ces films sont souvent associés, Warhol lui-même ne les a jamais regardés en entier et préférait que les spectateurs en fasse autant, allant et venant à leur guise. Ainsi, en fonction de la durée externe du temps de visionnement, ce mode de présentation offre un contraste saisissant avec la pratique des cinéastes structurels qui dépendaient du protocole de visionnement plus rigide, immobile imposé par la salle de cinéma. Plus précisément, le mode de réception d'un film comme *Sleep* s'oppose tant sur le plan phénoménologique que conceptuel à celui d'un film comme *La Région Centrale* (1971) de Michael Snow, qui exige un investissement de trois heures du temps du spectateur. L'œuvre de Snow s'articule autour de son effet de plus en plus vertigineux, hallucinant et brut sur le spectateur *captif*.

Bien qu'ils s'adressent à un spectateur immobile dans une salle de cinéma, les films de Snow n'en sont pas moins des exemples des pratiques filmiques radicales des années 60 et du début des années 70. Cela dit Snow se distingue par l'élaboration de sa critique à l'égard de l'illusionisme filmique et des modalités du temps filmique. Son film *See you Later/Au Revoir* (1990), d'une durée de 18 minutes, met en scène le plus banal des non-événements (un homme quittant un bureau). En photographiant l'action à un rythme de plusieurs milliers de cadres par seconde, Snow réussit à la ralentir presque au point de l'immobiliser. Cette distension extrême d'une action d'environ 30 secondes investit ce geste banal d'une remarquable qualité sculpturale à la limite du suspense. En re-présentant la continuité temporelle d'un moment narratif aussi éphémère et arbitraire – un moment qui, par convention, serait subsumer sous le système formel de la rupture de continuité dans un film grand public – dans des conditions aussi concrètes et palpables de temps filmique, Snow donne un nouveau sens à la pénétration chirurgicale que Walter Benjamin associe au travail du caméraman en ce qui concerne le sujet enregistré[20]. *See You Later/Au revoir* pousse cette pénétration métaphorique à l'extrême, transformant une action brève, et par ailleurs banale, en un spectacle quasi fantasmagorique.

Les artistes contemporains ont élaborés une vaste gamme de stratégies qui semblent donner suite aux objectifs critiques du cinéma d'avant-garde, reproduisant et remettant en question les différentes conditions historiques du rapport spectateur-spectacle du cinéma. À la base de cette orientation, comme je l'ai déja mentionné, se trouve un éventail de travaux théoriques qui mettent en corrélation les normes et conventions changeantes du cinéma contemporain et la réception filmique avec les permutations instables des débuts de la culture visuelle moderne où le cinéma n'était qu'une forme – particulièrement fascinante nous en convenons – technologique et culturelle parmi d'autres[21]. Comme l'ont fait valoir Leo Charney et Vanessa R. Schwartz : «Le cinéma n'était qu'un élément parmi une multitude de nouveaux modes de technologie, de représentation, de spectacle, de distraction, de consommation, d'éphémère, de mobilité et de divertissement, et à de nombreux égards il n'était ni le plus fascinant ni le plus prometteur[22]. » L'avènement du nouvel historicisme comme méthode d'analyse des débuts du cinéma dans la culture moderne reflète un intérêt plus vaste pour les différents modes de conscience et formules de subjectivité dans lesquels s'inscrivent le cinéma et les formes de temps filmique.

Cette hypothèse pourrait être soulignée en partie par la prédominance dans les films et les vidéos des figures, structures formelles et techniques de mise en scène de la durée, qui se réclament en général du cinéma primitif, du cinéma d'avant-garde des années 60 et 70 et de la narratologie moderniste européenne. D'où le rôle de premier plan joué par Warhol dans l'établissement de liens entre les pratiques filmiques d'avant-garde des années 60 et le cinéma d'exposition de l'art contemporain. Contrairement à bon nombre de ses contemporains qui ont abandonné la peinture pour la sculpture au début des années 60, Warhol s'est tourné vers le cinéma. Le souci de Warhol pour la littéralité engendrée par l'extrême longueur de ses films et leurs temps morts offre une expérience de visionnement que Margulies considère hyperréaliste dans sa littéralité.

Selon elle, le cinéma hyperréaliste de Warhol suppose une problématique, voire même une remise en question, de l'épistémologie qui sous-tend les modes littéraux et figuratifs de la représentation filmique en général. Dans un environnement médiatique saturé de divertissements populaires qui réunissent réalité et représentation, et dont l'emploi du temps reflète les catégories génériques changeantes des débuts du cinéma, le recours au temps littéral par l'art contemporain peut être perçu comme une tentative pour atténuer la séduction illusoire de ces nouveaux forums culturels. Fondamentalement, ces stratégies se résument à la mise en scène du temps filmique sans recours aucun aux matériaux, techniques et répertoire du cinéma. Par exemple, *24-Hour Psycho* de Douglas Gordon inscrit le temps filmique dans une sorte d'animation suspendue, utilisant (paradoxalement) un magnétoscope et une copie VHS du *Psycho* d'Hitchcock. Une œuvre comme celle-là fait ressortir l'arbitraire des caractéristiques matérielles et des contextes de réception du cinéma dans l'élaboration de mises en scène de la durée.

Mettant à contribution ces diverses conceptions du temps filmique, l'art contemporain réactualise (et non seulement réitère) la critique de l'avant-garde de l'illusionnisme filmique en présentant, à un spectateur désormais habitué à manipuler des images animées, une configuration qui refuse délibérément cette possibilité d'exagérer et d'intensifier la qualité non-maîtrisable du temps filmique. Cela se produit par le biais de permutations de la durée réalisées à l'aide de dispositifs tels que des écrans ou des canaux multiples, des projections en boucle et des séances de visionnement à heures fixes dans les galeries. Les cinéastes hollandais de Rijke et de Rooij présentent fréquemment leurs films dans des galeries à heures fixes, préférant que les spectateurs regardent chacun des films en entier. Dans leur installation intitulée *Bantar Gebang* (2000), la durée se présente comme une sorte d'hésitation phénoménologique entre la fixité et le mouvement de l'image photographique ; cette rencontre – créée dans le contexte d'une expérience muséale qui évoque explicitement les conventions du cinéma traditionnel – semble entraîner, de par son protocole de visionnement, une forme d'immersion contemplative.

Mon intention ici n'était pas simplement de réaffirmer l'argument souvent répété voulant que le cinéma d'avant-garde des années 60 se réfère par atavisme aux débuts du cinéma dans ses conditions formelles et esthétiques, et que les pratiques contemporaines du film et de la vidéo continuent dans cette lignée. Plutôt j'ai tenté de mettre en valeur certains des éventuels points de référence théoriques, auxquels ont recours les œuvres contemporaines pour réactualiser d'anciens modèles de réception filmique dans leur usage de la durée. Si, comme l'ont suggéré des théoriciens du cinéma, ces qualités mutables de la durée nous force à revoir les assises conceptuelles des formes filmiques de la rhétorique visuelle, ou l'épistémologie même de l'image filmique, alors l'afflux de pratiques filmiques dans les musées laisse à penser que nous avons épuisé les lieux propices à un échange critique entre le spectateur et l'image filmique. Que l'espace public et la télévision, comme éventuels sites de diffusion, soient trop monopolisés par la publicité pour se prêter à la réflexion critique semble suggérer que le musée demeure le seul endroit où les conditions phénoménologiques et esthétiques de l'image animée puissent être débattues. Il s'agit peut-être de l'horizon qui permettra au cinéma d'exposition de récupérer une forme de potentiel critique.

NOTES

1. Jacques Aumont, « L'Œil variable, ou la mobilisation du regard », in *L'Œil interminable : cinéma et peinture*, Paris, Librairie Séguier, 1989, p. 58.

2. Voir par exemple Emmanuel Hermange, « Pour nous le cinéma est mort : Notes sur quelques stratégies cinéphiles de l'art » *Parachute* n° 103, (07-08-09/2001), p.12-25.

3. Nous pourrions comparer le double mouvement du cinéma à celui de la photographie. D'aucuns suggèrent que les progrès de l'imagerie numérique et la prolifération des images qui s'ensuit annoncent un avenir « post-photographique » où aucune image ne saura prétendre à la « vérité visuelle » du fait de son rapport indexical à une « réalité » pré-existante. Inversement, la réinterprétation de l'émergence de la

photographie remet en question la notion d'indexicalité en tant que caractéristique intrinsèque de l'élaboration d'une épistémologie photographique à ses débuts. Voir à ce sujet, William J. Mitchell, *The Reconfigured Eye: Visual Truth in the Post-Photographic Era,* Cambridge, Mass. et Londres, MIT Press, 1992, et Geoffrey Batchen, *Burning With Desire: The Conception of Photography,* Cambridge, Mass. et Londres, MIT Press, 1997.

4. Aumont, *op.cit.* p. 52.

5. Voir notamment *Early Cinema: Space, Frame, Narrative*, sous la direction de Thomas Elsaesser, Londres, BFI, 1990.

6. Aumont, *op.cit.* p. 52.

7. Voir Jonathan Crary, *Suspensions of Perception: Attention, Spectacle and Modern Culture,* Cambridge, Mass. et Londres, MIT Press, 1999.

8. Aumont, *op.cit.* p. 60.

9. Aumont, *op.cit.* p. 72.

10. *Ibid.* 58.

11. Pour une discussion du rapport entre l'art moderne et le cinéma expérimental des années 60 et 70 d'un point de vue temporel et théâtral, voir Ivone Margulies, « Toward a Corporeal Cinema », *Nothing Happens: Chantal Ackerman's Hyperrealist Everyday,* Durham, NC, et Londres, Duke University Press, 1996, p. 42-64.

12. Aumont, *op.cit.* p. 63.

13. Mary Ann Doane, *The Emergence of Cinematic Time: Modernity, Contingency, the Archive,* Cambridge, Mass. et Londres, Harvard University Press, 2002.

14. *Ibid.*, p. 140-141.

15. Cité dans Jim Hoberman, « After Avant-Garde Film », dans Brian Wallis, sous la dir., Art After Modernism: Rethinking Representation, New York, New Museum of Contemporary Art; Boston, D.R. Godine, 1984, p. 63.

16. *Ibid.*

17 Ivone Margulies, *Nothing Happens,* p. 37.

18. *Ibid.*, p. 38.

19. *Ibid.*

20. Walter Benjamin, « L'Œuvre d'art à l'époque de sa reproduction mécanisée » rééd. dans *Écrits français*, Paris, Gallimard, 1991.

21. Voir Leo Charney et Vanessa R. Schwartz (sous la dir.), *Cinema and the Invention of Modern Life*, Berkeley, University of California Press, 1995 ; Anne Friedberg, *Window Shopping: Cinema and the Postmodern,* Berkeley et Los Angeles, University of California Press, 1993.

22. Leo Charney et Vanessa R. Schwartz, « Introduction », *Cinema and the Invention of Modern Life*, p. 1.

WORK

OEUVR

ES

Artist / Artiste
PASCAL GRANDMAISON

Title / Titre
***Spin*, 2002**
Support
DVD projection
Projection DVD
Duration / Durée
16 minutes looped
16 minutes en boucle

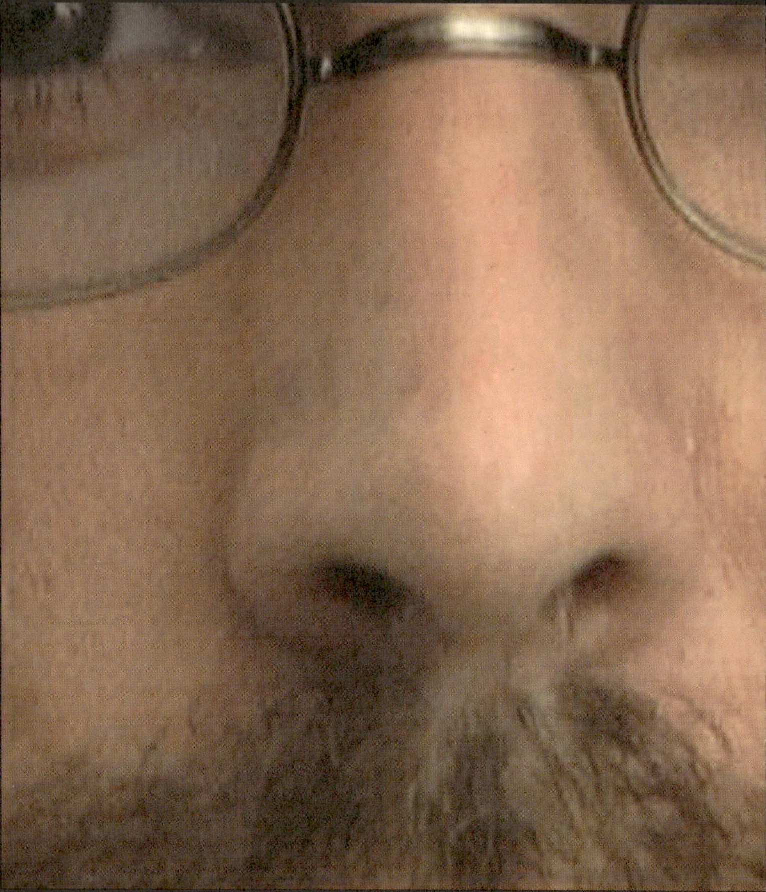

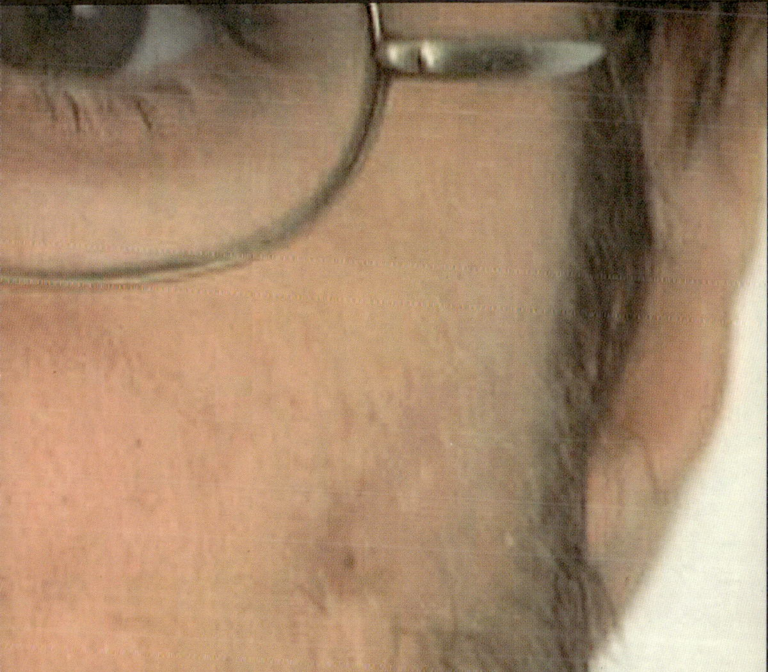

Artist / Artiste
ANDY WARHOL

Title / Titre
Screen Tests, 1963 - 1966
Support
16 mm black and white film
transferred to DVD
Film 16 mm noir et blanc
transféré sur DVD
Duration / Durée
4 min., each at 16 frames
per second
4 min, 16 plans seconde

Screen Test: Ann Buchanan,
1964
Screen Test: Marcel Duchamp,
1966

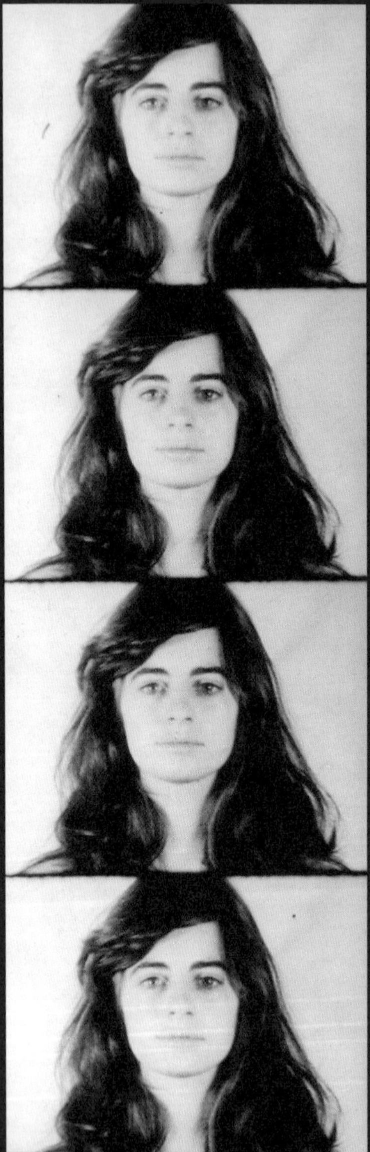

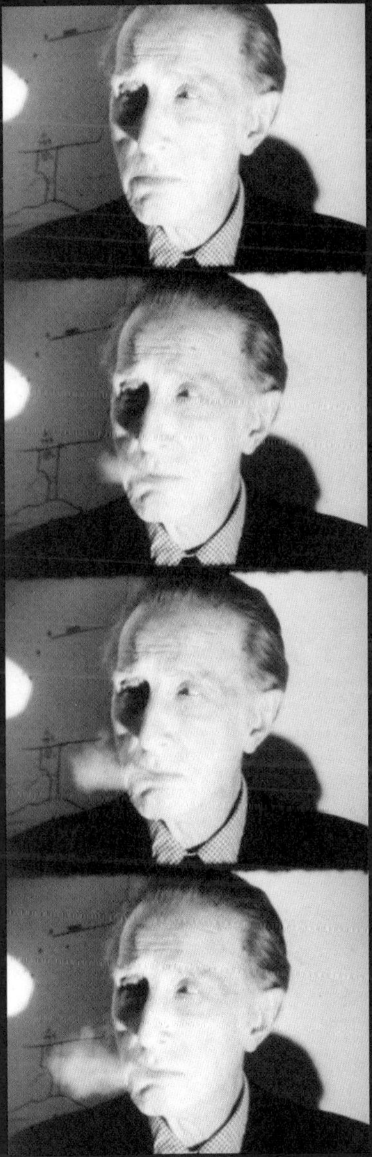

Artist / Artiste
JOCELYN ROBERT

Title / Titre
Catarina, 2002
Support
DVD projection with sound
Projection DVD avec son
Duration / Durée
9 minutes looped
9 minutes en boucle

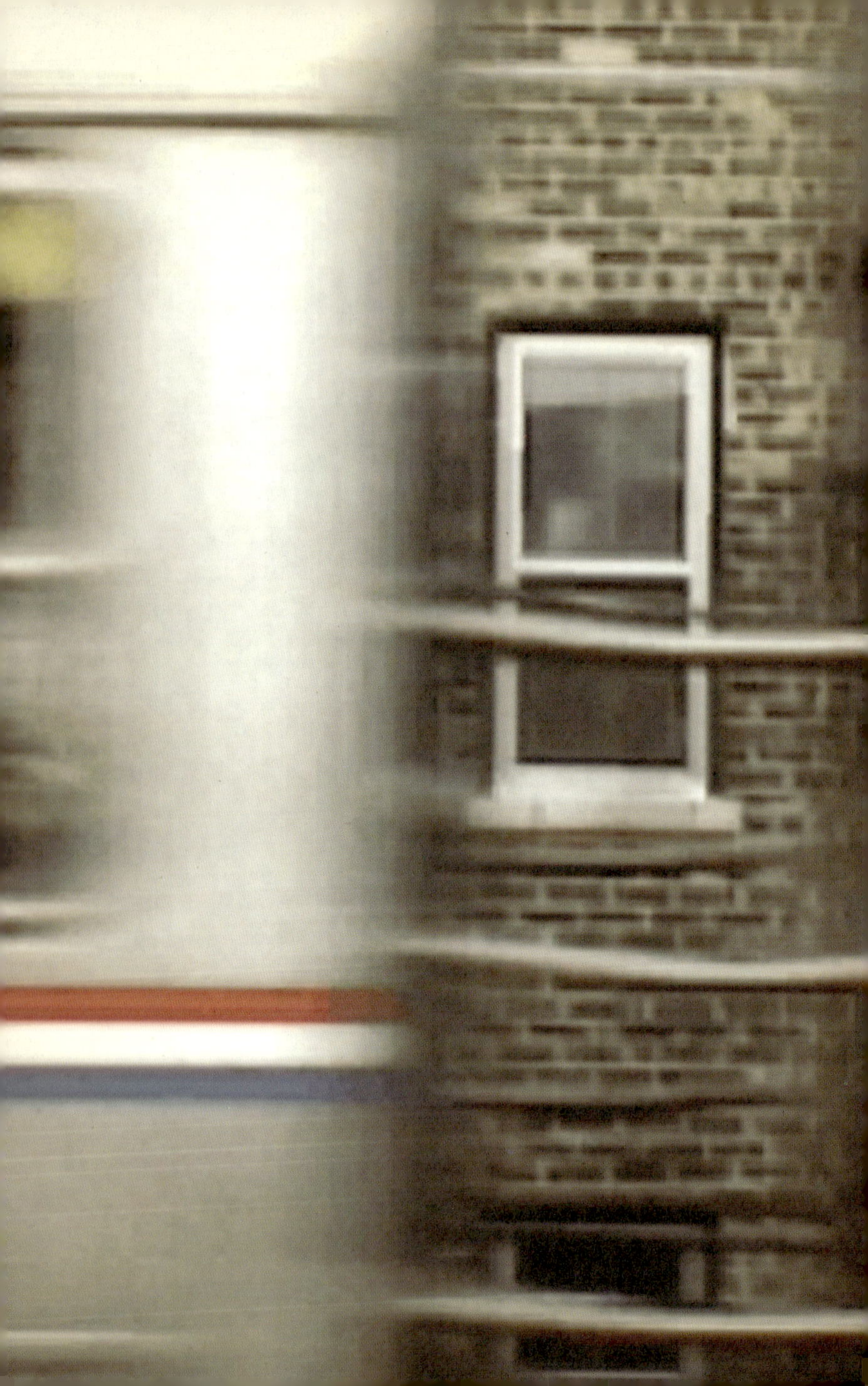

Artist / Artiste
MICHAEL SNOW

Title / Titre
One Second in Montreal, 1969
Support
16 mm black and white film
Film 16 mm en noir et blanc
Duration / Durée
26 minutes

Title / Titre
Side Seat Slides Paintings Sound Film, 1970
Support
16 mm colour film with sound
Film 16 mm en couleur avec son
Duration / Durée
20 minutes

Title / Titre
See You Later/Au revoir, 1990
Support
16 mm colour film with sound
Film 16 mm en couleur avec son
Duration / Durée
18 minutes

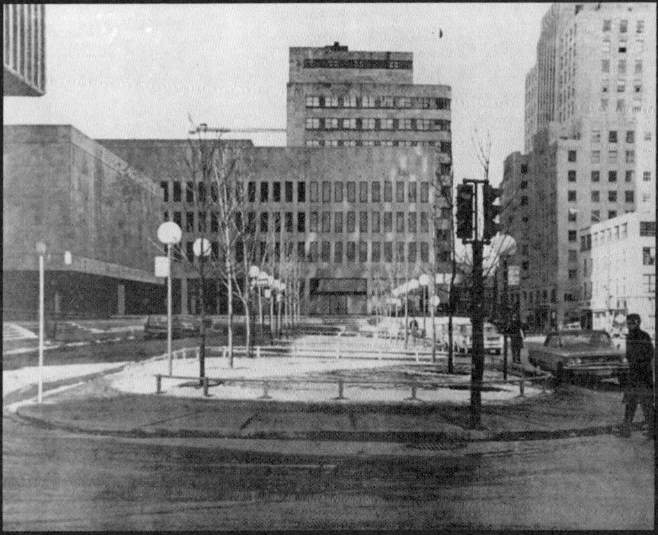

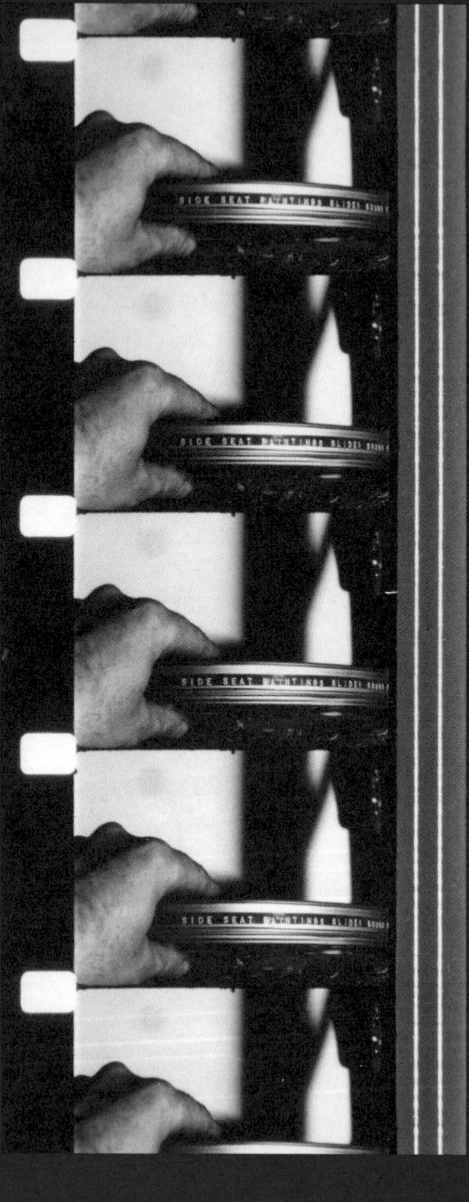
SIDE SEAT

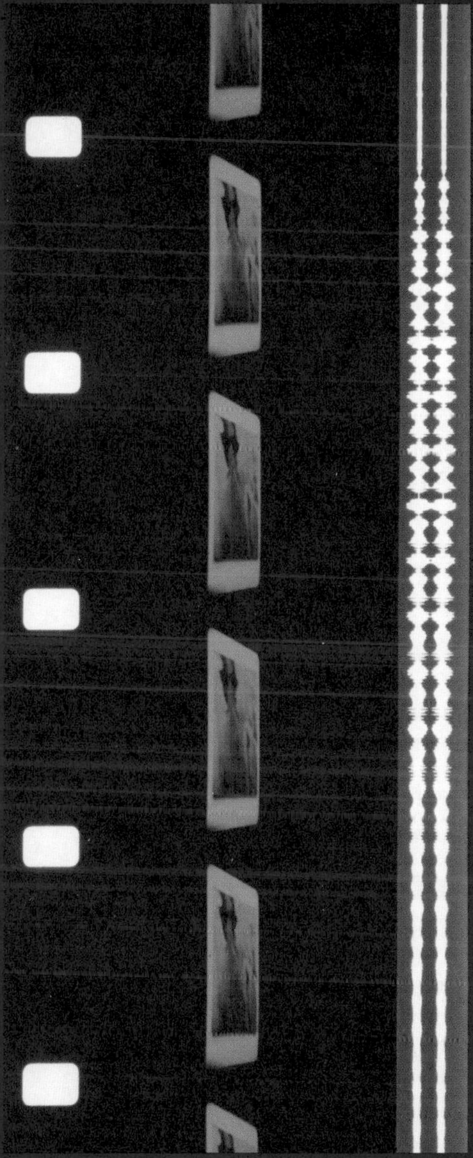

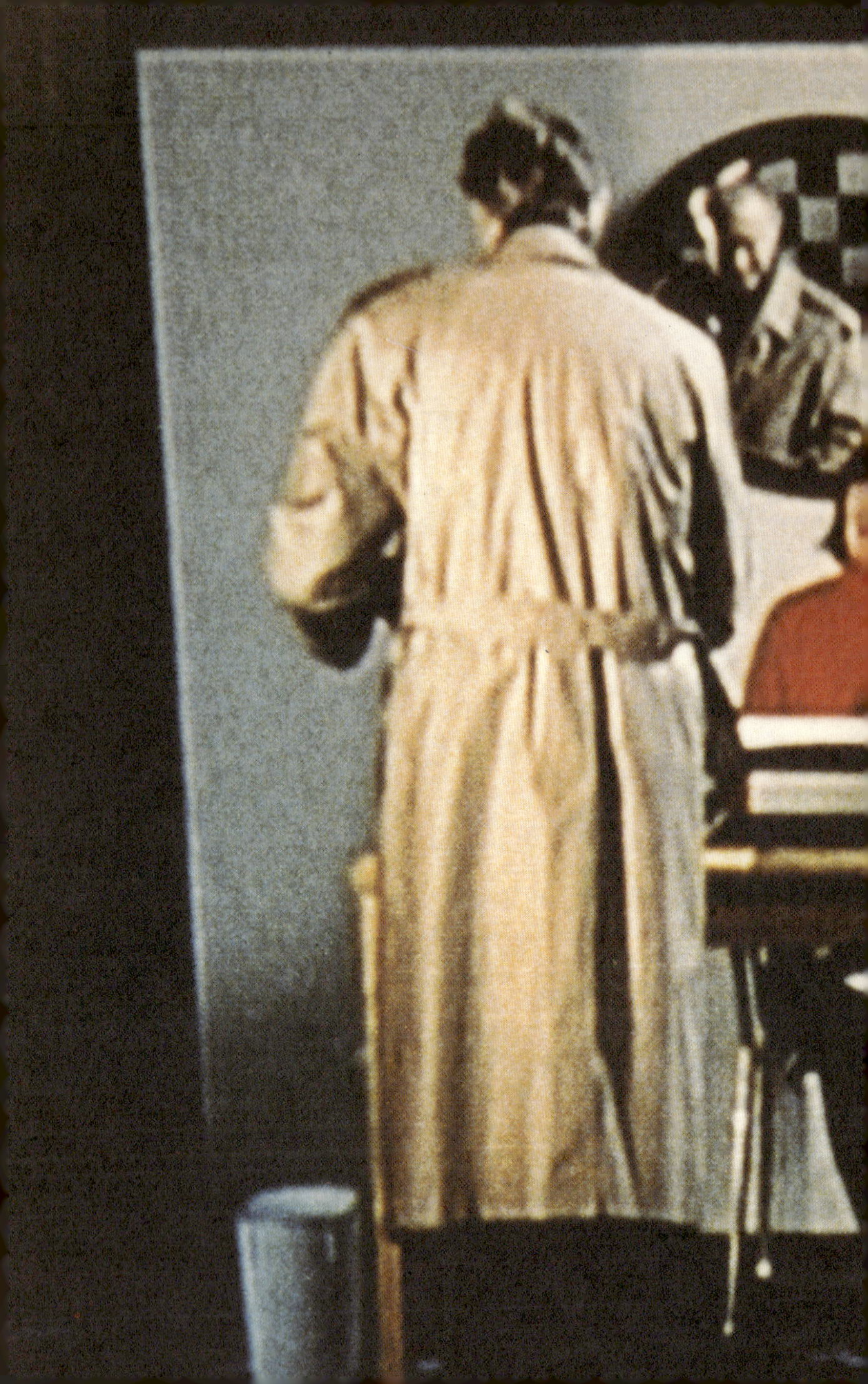

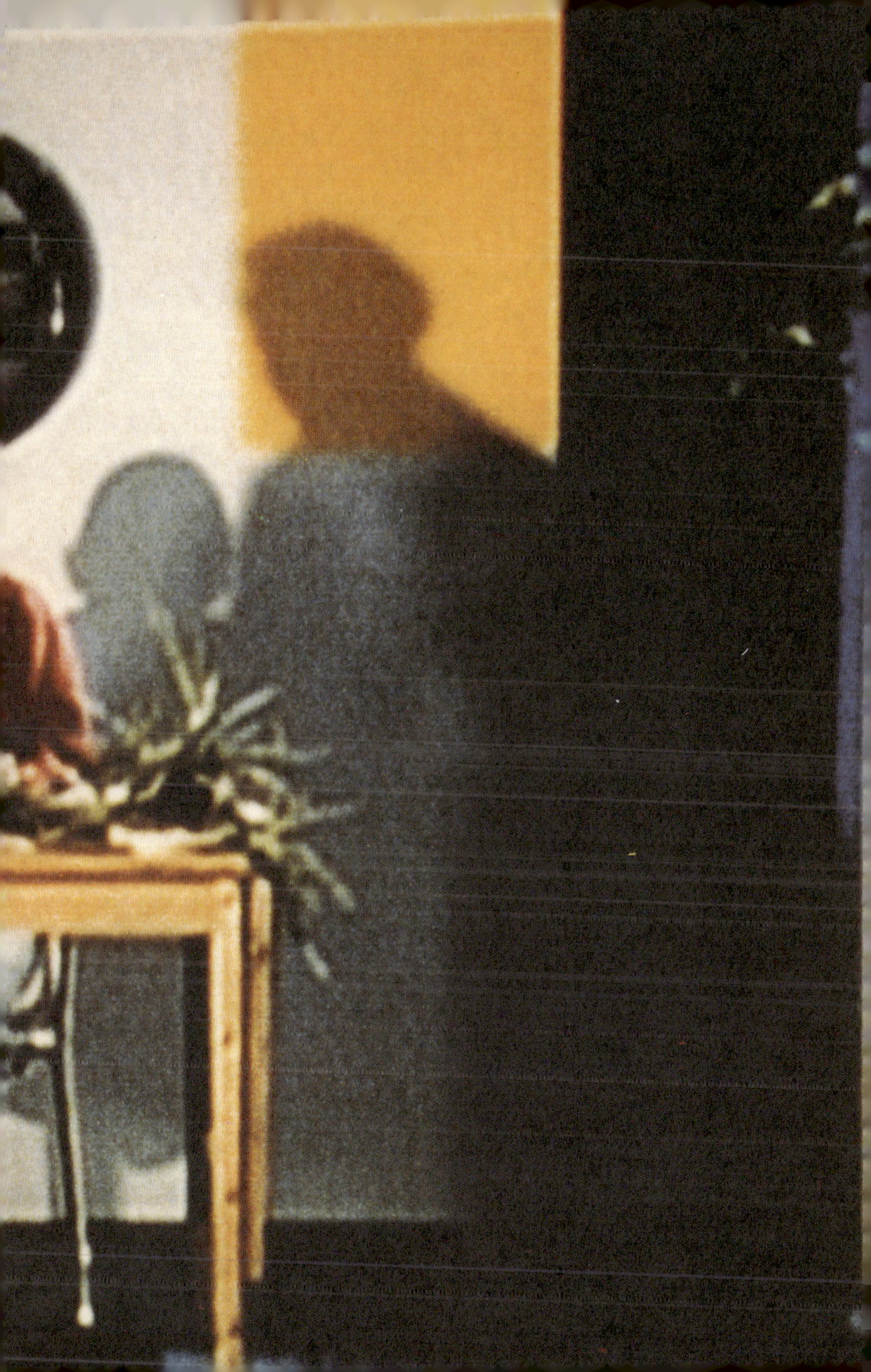

Artist / Artiste
GWEN MACGREGOR

Title / Titre
***Up to the 8th floor*, 2004**
Support
Triptych. DVD projection
Triptyque. Projection DVD
Duration / Durée
Looped / En boucle

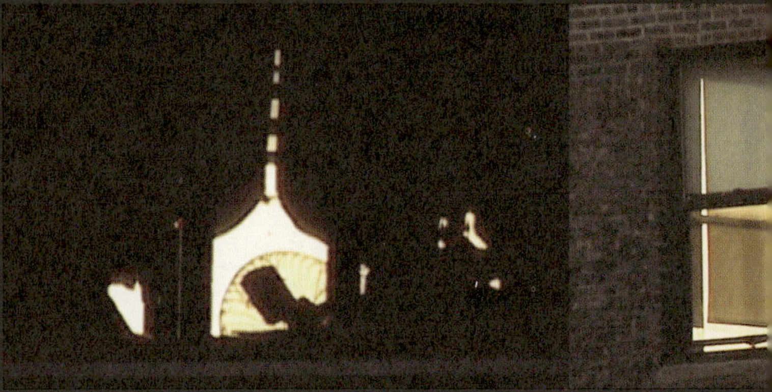

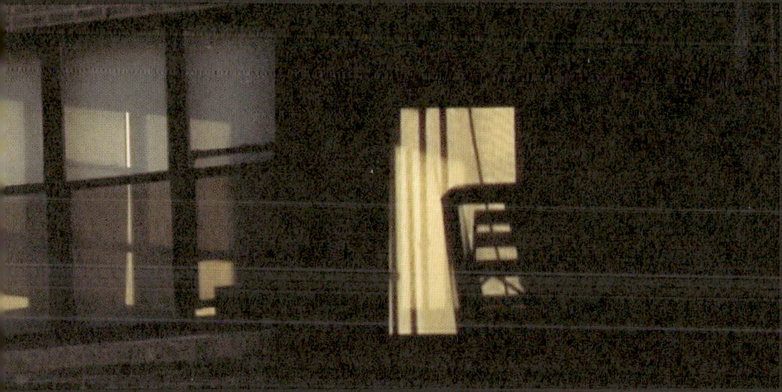

Artist / Artiste
JEROEN DE RIJKE / WILLEM DE ROOIJ

Title / Titre
Bantar Gebang, 2000
Support
35 mm color film with optical sound
Film 35 mm en couleur avec son optique
Duration / Durée
10 minutes

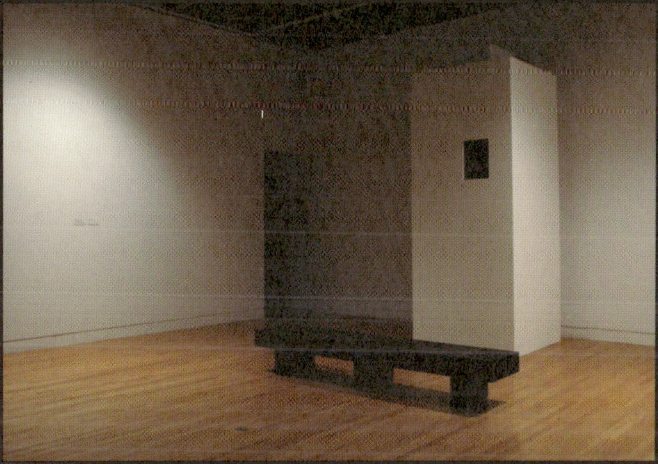

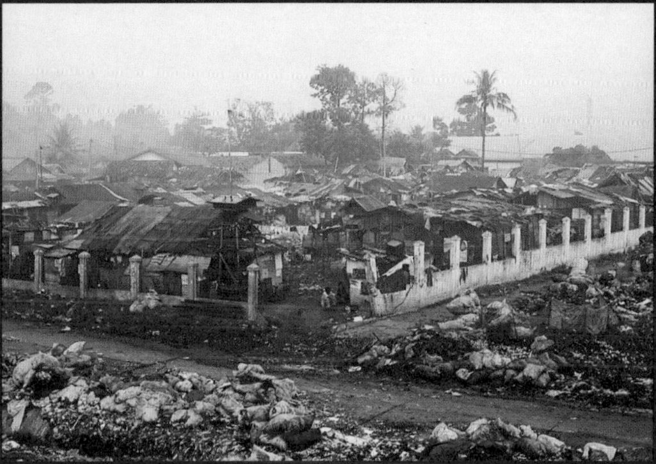

I'm moving forward while thinking backward, or is it moving backward while thinking forward? Either way my work has a push-me/pull-you relationship with time. I make installations and video that embrace the ordinary event, the overlooked evidence of time and place. Sometimes the work is site-specific and uses ephemeral materials in conjunction with the architectural history of the site. Other works are gallery-based and use time-based elements like video and sound. In all cases there is a gathering of elements that is about a commitment to process, and the development of meaning through that process. The resulting works allow for a slow discovery and transformation of the ordinary moment, seeping into the audience's eyes and ears. My work offers a kind of present day traveling.

Gwen MacGregor

On imagine facilement le temps qui passe comme une rivière qui coule. C'est une image employée par de nombreux poètes. Mais le premier marin venu vous dira que l'eau ne coule jamais de manière constante, sans histoire. Il y a toujours de petits tourbillons, des remous, des courants ... il peut même arriver que l'eau remonte la rivière en un point donné. Dans certaines de mes installations, c'est un peu le genre de lieu que je cherche à créer : j'essaie de creuser de petites alcôves dans le temps qui passe.

Jocelyn Robert

PLEASE TAKE THE TIME TO READ ALL OF THIS

Film is the first representational medium to guarantee specific durations to the user.

Film cameras and projectors are members of the clock family.

Metronome markings in music scores (an attempt at an agreement as to the duration of individual notes in a specific piece) are a predecessor. But performance is subject to human whim.

In film projection a shutter isolates each frame. There are 24 frames per second, a frame (a single photograph) = $1/24^{th}$ of a second.

The visible (to some) pulse of a projected film is caused by the shutter, by the back and forth between one forty-eighth of a second of dark followed by one forty-eighth of a second of projected image.

This really is a "pulse", a "heart-beat" which, mechanically regular, tick-tocks *in* the image, the passing of time.

An interesting difference between projected film and projected digital video is the latter's unmodulated glare. It is more difficult for a digital image to communicate duration. In the compression algorithm of a digital image only what changes in the shot is renewed. Pixel based images are more "graphic" than sensorial. Even film grain resembles our eyes' rods and cones. But digital video has its own interesting qualities.

As an artist I work for and with the qualities and contexts of mediums. In 1970, I made *Sink* a continuous-play carousel slide gallery work. My *De La* is one of the first real-time video installations. *Two Sides to Every Story* is a gallery film installation of 1974, currently in the Whitney Museum's touring exhibition *Into the Light*.

I have made several digital video works: the 90 minute cinema-theatre **Corpus Callosum* (2000) and the continuous-play DVD gallery installation, *That/Cela/Dat* (2000), *Sheeploop* (2001) and *Solar Breath (Northern Caryatids)* (2002).

For the exhibition accompanying this catalogue, Michèle Thériault has chosen 3 of my very specifically cinema-theatre works, that is, they were composed for the cinema-theatre, the church/theatre relative which physically is a room with seats set before a screen with a projector room behind the spectator and which socially/psychologically requests a trusting agreement/commitment as to, precisely, duration, from those who have chosen to seat themselves.

One Second in Montreal (1969) is a silent film which is purely made of durations. The images are filmings of not-very-well-done offset printings of still photographs.

The film is constructed solely of holds of mathematically determined lengths. As the film progresses the holds get longer and longer, using the Fibonacci series (for example if the first hold was 134 frames then the next would be 213 frames and the next would be 347 frames etc.).

30 still photographs (perhaps taken at 1/30th of a second) of Montreal parks under snow are used.

After the longest hold (the 15th, I think) the holds start to progressively shorten using another mathematical series (no holds in the film are the same length) until the last photo is only one frame.

This work can only be understood by seeing it in its entirety, by experiencing it.

The long title *Side Seat Paintings Slides Sound Film* is explicit. It was shot as if from a bad (too far to the side) seat in a cinema-theatre. What the side-seated camera saw was the carousel projection of a series of slides of various paintings. Perhaps it was an art history lecture or a slide projection of some of his paintings by Michael Snow, whose voice can be heard giving the title, date, medium and dimensions of each painting, all of which, as projected in the film, are totally unrelated to their real sources, sizes per slide are all different and the "side-seat" view makes it hard to make the paintings out anyway.

The carousel projections were all the same 15 seconds, but the filming speed was varied, making the whole thing slow down. The voice deepens and the image darkens. Then, it all speeds up as if during a lecture you nodded off and woke with a start.

See You Later / Au Revoir also uses the possibility of changing the speed of the action in the image. The real-time action (a man puts on a coat and leaves an office, pausing to say goodbye to a typing secretary) took 30 seconds but the entire scene (built on a single right to left tripod pan) was slowed down to 17 minutes. This was made in 1990.

Traditionally a museum/art gallery visit is a promenade. The flexible relationship of the walker/viewer/spectator to a "painting" remains the norm.

Kinetic work, especially moving images must consider (and/or create) the physical context. Inevitably gallery projections must be looped and non-developmental, one should be able to "enter" them at anytime and still get something from the work (again the viewer/painting paradigm where the duration of viewing is entirely the spectator's choice).

It took me 2 hours to write this and 5 minutes and 40 seconds to read it.

August 2004

Michael Snow

THOUGHTS ON "EXHIBITION CINEMA"

Michèle Thériault

The predominant discourse in the proliferation of exhibitions featuring the moving image is, certainly, the one that links this type of image and its mode of presentation to cinematographic culture. "Exhibition cinema," as it is dubbed, stands apart from cinema proper – the other cinema – by its eschewing of theatre-based screenings, the increased mobility afforded the viewers who are no longer required to remain seated, the continuous presence of the moving image (video projections are, for the most part, looped sequences), the frequent use of multiple screens to create an immersive environment, and, last but not least, the exploration of narrative and figurative modes and of shooting methods specific to cinema.

Cinematographic culture, which goes back to Edison's and the Lumière brothers first flickerings in the late 19th century, was profoundly shaken in the 20th century by the arrival of television and large-scale advertising (including music video spin-offs). So much so, that it has become difficult to separate these three areas one from the other. Moreover, technological advances in video and digitalization and a host of ever more sophisticated softwares have eroded the specificity of the cinematographic act and redefined the nature of the filmed image, while fostering the development of amateur cinema and a certain democratization of cinema itself. Clearly, then, a great number of factors combine to create a "cinema effect" in exhibitions of contemporary art.

These characteristics are necessarily mobile themselves because the infiltration of cinema into the culture and history of the image within art institutions has blurred the boundary between cinema and the visual arts and set new parameters for visitor experience. The discourse developed around artistic practices of the moving image and their site of exhibition is unfixed and multifaceted. The diversity and crossovers of image-producing and projecting devices used by artists has created works and an experience whose hybridity points, as Raymond Bellour has suggested, to an aesthetics of confusion.[1] One relationship, however, is inevitably reconsidered in all exhibitions involving video or film projections, and that is the visitor's relationship to time. Philip Monk is correct when he says that it is not a question of new media but of a changed relation to time, no matter what the medium.[2]

It is more constructive, therefore, to consider this mode of art from the viewpoint of a precise context and conditions, rather than trying to circumscribe it within general terms – particularly since it is by nature resistant to such attempts, having not yet ceased to transform itself, visitor experience and the nature of the space in which it it is presented. *Timelength* discusses specific issues within precise parameters. It brings together works that delve into specific aspects of this "other cinema" from the vantage point of duration, which is articulated within a sort of oppositional tension: slowness-quasi-fixedness-immobility /acceleration-movement-mobility; silence / sound; video / film; monitor / projector; temporality / atemporality; darkness / light.

This exhibition would also like to reflect upon "exhibition cinema" by having visitors experience distinct modes of image production and presentation, namely, 16mm and 35mm film, projected in their original formats; film works transferred to DVD; and video projection. It was important to relate the question of duration and its rendering by young artists like Pascal Grandmaison, Gwen MacGregor and Jocelyn Robert by juxtaposing their work to the films of Michael Snow and Andy Warhol and their singular exploration of duration within the moving image. Starting in the 1960s, each of these two artists, in a distinctive way, significantly broadened the nature of film experience. Snow's films explore duration as an inherent property of the film process, while Warhol's are inscribed within the iconic and popular culture of cinema.

In no way am I advocating the separation of media in order to preserve some putative purity specific to each. Rather, I want to highlight the image's complexity in the simple variations that it undergoes through the means used to capture and present it. As visitors come face to face with images possessing varied textures and resolutions, a problematic begins to take shape within the fluctuations of the image itself and of one's experience of it. To view a 16mm film by Michael Snow is to experience a graininess of image scored now and then by the trembling shape of a dust particle, an image that is slightly unstable for having been spliced and hence always bound to the apparatus that projects it. The same holds for the 35mm image of artists like de Rijke and de Rooij, which possesses exceptional definition and clarity. Durations produced by film and video are inherently different. "In a film", Snow says,"the shutter isolates each frame. The visible (to some) pulse of a projected film is caused by the shutter, by the back and forth between one forty-eighth of a second of dark followed by one forty-eighth of a second of projected image." This back and forth, Snow adds, is like a pulse marking time. Because of its lack of modulation and its algorithmic compression, the projected digital image has a harder time conveying duration.[3] Moreover because they arise out of a chemical process and consequently do not possess video's potential for immediacy, film images are somewhat immune to this profound effect of enhanced reality, to that excess of the real, suggestive of simulation, that emanates from the video image. The film image bears the time of its "coming into being" within itself, unlike today's video image, which, in its unceasing and inexorable electronic presence, seems entirely devoid of a past. But it is in this continuous present, which is, so to speak, outside time, that "videographic" duration is constituted. Yet a film today can be entirely digitally simulated and the differences in the way duration exists in film and video are no longer the sole property of each medium as one bleeds into the other.

If the discourse on "exhibition cinema" and even exhibitions themselves seems to privilege a relationship with the culture of popular cinema and large-scale, ultra-designed urban advertising, *Timelength*, without wanting to suppress its latent presence in certain works – namely Grandmaison's *Spin* – would like experimental cinema, its culture and strategies, its overturning of popular film codes and *mise en abîme* of its own processes to circulate in and around the works presented.

Andy Warhol and, particularly, Michael Snow were part of an experimental film culture that assimilated their work from a critical perspective. This community, which Snow describes as secret in its relationship with the art world, remains marginalized – few gallery goers know it well – but it was there, over the course of the 20th century, that film, the moving image and its temporality would undergo profound transformations and a constant re-evaluation. The productions that emerged from this culture – one thinks of Snow's *Wavelength* and *La région centrale* and Warhol's *Empire* – are radical experiments of duration within the image. Even if visitors to exhibitions are generally conversant with popular cinema and in many instances remain ignorant of experimental film culture, it was important that the radicality it represents permeates the exhibition. Oddly, works constituted of projected images possess a "spectacular" character akin to that of popular cinema, especially the films produced by Hollywood, but their critical questioning of this culture resides with investigations characteristic of experimental and alternative cinema.

Timelength engages visitors in a frontal encounter with the work. The decision to leave out multi-screen projections was deliberate so that the relationship to the still fixed image and the pictorial as such, could be looked at more closely. By "exhibiting" the moving image, *Timelength* inscribes itself in an exhibition history marked by the fixed image and, indeed, by painting. Moreover, the slowness and fixedness inherent to works included here (which extends time and transforms them, in the process, into durational works), plays off the contemplative relationship characteristic of "pictures" and their fixed image. It is not a matter of assimilating "exhibition cinema" to the pictorial continuum – for the former undoubtedly upsets the latter; rather what needs to be examined is "the meaning and manifestations of this reversal of the mobile into the motionless."[4] In fact, it is hoped that *Timelength* will help to call the very identity of every image into question, along with its precariousness, whether it is fixed and on a substantial material support like that of a painting, or whether it is mobile and immaterial, as in a projection.[5]

While the visitor's relationship to the works in *Timelength* is frontal, this does not mean that their experience requires immobility from the viewer. Even though the films of Snow and de Rijke / de Rooij require the visitor to seat him or herself before a predetermined screening, the semi-visible space of presentation, once the projector has been shut down, becomes a place of scrutinizing mobility. In the looped wall projections of Grandmaison, MacGregor and Robert, visitors are no longer bound to conventional cinema viewing and can move as they please. In the discourse on exhibition-based cinema, the question of radicality is linked to the visitor's mobility in his or her relationship to the moving image. However, to equate mobility, liberty and radicality on the one hand, and immobility, passivity and conventionality on the other, as is often the case, is to simplify the issue of the reception of works of art, and to overlook a whole range of other factors that work to shape it. [6] It is, therefore, much more productive to envision the advent of the moving and projected image (along with the emergence of non-optical sensory practices) in museums and other exhibition venues as a means of rethinking the tensions continually at play between viewer and art work, whatever the latter may be. In this way one can have so-called "conventional" modes of reception participate in a contemporaneous discourse.

In conclusion, I would like to bring to the fore the practice of reading (particularly of fictional narratives) to open a breach in the discourse on the cinematic spectacular as a way of thinking differently about what one sees (and hears). Reading is a practice conspicuously marked by duration and one that confines a being to specific durations. It is in the way that it (particularly the reading of fictional narrative) absorbs body and mind, the temporal discrepancies that it produces in the ensuing rupture with the world, the intimate and concentrated nature of its hold on our imagination and on our perception and our senses (that compels us constantly to readjust to reality), that its experience becomes inscribed in the calibrated sphere of the illuminated image that visitors to exhibitions watch in the dark.

NOTES

1. Raymond Bellour, "Battle of the Images," *Art Press,* no. 262 (Nov. 2000): 52. An example of this aesthetic of confusion is found in Janet Cardiff and George Bures Miller's *The Paradise Institute*. The work is presented inside a box that replicates a movie theatre with projection booth and rows of seating.

2. Philip Monk, "Paint it Black: Curating the Temporal Image," *Prefix*, no. 9 (May 2004): 17-18.

3. Michael Snow, "Please Take the Time to Read All of This," 2004. Reproduced in this catalogue, p. 99.

4. Jean-Christophe Royoux, "Cinema as Exhibition, Duration as Space," *Art Press*, no. 262 (Nov. 2000): 40.

5. Boris Groys, "On the Aesthetics of Video Installations," *Stan Douglas: Le Détroit*, exhibition catalogue (Basel: Kunsthalle Basel, 2001).

6. Mark Nash, "Art and Cinema: Some Critical Reflections, *Documenta 11*; *Platform V: Exhibition Catalogue* (Ostfildern-Ruit: Hatje Cantz, 2002), p. 129-133.

QUELQUES RÉFLEXIONS SUR « LE CINÉMA D'EXPOSITION »

Michèle Thériault

Le discours qui domine les nombreuses expositions mettant en scène l'image en mouvement est certainement celui qui lie ce type d'image et son mode de diffusion à la culture cinématographique. Qualifié de « cinéma d'exposition » il se distinguerait de « l'autre » cinéma par son abandon de la séance de projection dans une salle de théâtre, la mobilité accrue du spectateur qui n'est plus tenu de s'immobiliser dans un fauteuil, la présentation en continu de l'image en mouvement (les projections vidéo étant pour la plupart des séquences en boucle), l'usage fréquent d'écrans multiples créant une expérience immersive, et bien sûr l'exploration des modes narratifs et de figuration, et des modes de tournage propres au cinéma.

Cette culture qui remonte aux premiers scintillements de l'image d'Edison et des Frères Lumière à la fin du 19e siècle a été bouleversée au 20e siècle par l'avènement de la télévision et par la publicité (et ses dérivés les vidéoclips). Si bien qu'aujourd'hui ces trois champs ne sont plus distincts. Les avancées technologiques de la vidéo, du numérique et de toute une gamme de logiciels ont par ailleurs ébranlé la spécificité de l'acte cinématographique, brouillé la définition de l'image filmique, tout en alimentant le développement du cinéma amateur et d'une certaine démocratisation du cinéma. C'est donc dire que plusieurs facteurs influent sur « l'effet cinéma » dans les expositions d'art contemporain.

De toute évidence ces caractéristiques sont elles-mêmes mobiles car cette imbrication du cinéma dans la culture et l'histoire de l'image au sein du lieu muséal brouille les frontières et du cinéma et des arts visuels, et trace de nouvelles balises pour l'expérience du visiteur. Le champ de réflexion de ces pratiques qui jouent du cinéma et du lieu de leur déploiement est protéiforme et instable. Le croisement des dispositifs crée des œuvres et une expérience hybrides et mène, comme le suggère Raymond Bellour, à une esthétique de la confusion[1]. Mais il y a tout de même une relation qui est immanquablement repensée dans toutes ces expositions de projections et c'est celle que le visiteur entretient avec le temps. Philip Monk déclare à juste titre que ce n'est pas une question de nouveau média dans ce contexte mais d'un rapport transformé avec le temps peu importe le médium[2].

Il est donc plus sage de réfléchir à ce mode d'art à partir de conditions et d'un contexte précis au lieu d'essayer de le circonscrire en termes généraux, sa nature même s'y refusant car il n'a pas fini de se transformer et de transformer l'expérience du visiteur et la nature du lieu de sa présentation. *Timelength* élabore une réflexion à partir de paramètres précis. L'exposition rassemble des œuvres qui creusent des aspects particuliers de cet « autre cinéma » dans l'optique de la durée qui s'articule dans une espèce de tension oppositionnelle : lenteur-quasi-fixité-immobilité / mouvement-accélération-mobilité; silence / son; vidéo / film; moniteur / projection; temporalité / atemporalité; son / silence; obscurité / clarté.

L'exposition veut également mener à une réflexion sur le cinéma d'exposition en confrontant le visiteur à des modes distincts de production et de présentation de l'image à savoir le film 16mm et 35mm projeté dans sa forme originale, l'œuvre filmique transférée sur un support numérique et le vidéo et son projecteur. Il importait de mettre en rapport la question de la durée dans la production de jeunes artistes tels Pascal Grandmaison, Gwen MacGregor et Jocelyn Robert avec le traitement de la temporalité dans une production maintenant historique de l'image animée, en juxtaposant leur travail à celui de Michael Snow et d'Andy Warhol. À partir des années soixante ces deux artistes ont proposé selon un mode distinctif une définition élargie de l'expérience filmique. Les films de Snow explorent la durée comme propriété inhérente au processus filmique tandis que ceux de Warhol travaillent la durée dans la culture à la fois iconique et populaire du cinéma.

Je ne prône aucunement la séparation des médias afin de leur préserver une soi-disante pureté, mais je veux souligner la complexité de la question dans les simples variations que font subir à l'image son mode de captation et de diffusion. En mettant le visiteur en présence d'images possédant des textures et des définitions très variées une problématique se dessine dans les fluctuations de l'image elle-même et de son expérience. Visionner un film 16mm de Michael Snow c'est faire l'expérience d'une image granuleuse, traversée à certains moments par le profil tremblotant d'une poussière, légèrement instable parce qu'ayant subie un raccordement de plans, et, partant, toujours rattachée au dispositif qui nous la présente. Il en va de même pour l'image en 35mm des artistes de Rijke et de Rooij qui possède une qualité de définition et de clarté exceptionnelle. La durée produite par le film et la vidéo est différente. « Dans un film, commente Snow, l'obturateur isole chaque plan (frame). Le pouls visible (pour certains) d'un film projeté est dû à cet aller-retour entre un quarante-huitième de seconde de noirceur suivi par un quarante-huitième de seconde d'image projetée ». Cet aller-retour, ajoute Snow, est comme un battement qui marque le temps. Dans son absence de modulation et sa compression algorithmique l'image numérique projetée communiquerait plus difficilement la durée[3]. Par ailleurs, les images filmiques parce qu'elles sont produites sur pellicule, donc sans la possibilité d'immédiateté du processus vidéographique, échappent quelque peu à cet effet profond de réalité augmentée, à cet excès de réel suggérant une simulation qui se dégage de l'image vidéo. L'image filmique porte en elle le temps de sa mise au monde contrairement à celle produite aujourd'hui par la vidéo qui, dans sa présence électronique, continue et inexorable, semble ne posséder aucun passé. Mais, c'est dans ce présent continu, hors du temps pour ainsi dire, que se constitue la durée « vidéographique ».

Si le discours sur le cinéma d'exposition, voire les expositions elles-mêmes, semble privilégier un rapport avec la culture du cinéma populaire et de la publicité urbaine ultra design grand format, *Timelength*, sans vouloir étouffer sa présence latente dans certaines œuvres notamment *Spin* de Grandmaison, veut laisser planer, dans le sillage de l'exposition, la présence du cinéma expérimental, de ses stratégies, de son renversement des codes filmiques populaires et de sa mise en abîme de ses processus.

Andy Warhol et Michael Snow, plus particulièrement, ont évolué dans ce milieu qui a accueilli leurs films avec un esprit critique. Ce milieu que Snow qualifie de secret dans sa relation avec le milieu des arts, demeure marginalisé (peu de visiteurs aux expositions le connaissent bien) mais c'est bien là, au cours du xxe siècle, que le film, l'image animée et son temps furent l'objet de transformations profondes et d'une remise en question constante. Les productions de cette culture – on pense à *Wavelength* et à *La région centrale* de Snow ou à *Empire* de Warhol –, sont des expériences radicales de l'image de la durée. Même si le visiteur à l'exposition possède surtout une connaissance du cinéma populaire et demeure dans bien des cas ignorant de cette culture filmique il importe que cette radicalité traverse l'exposition, que sa présence soient notée. Curieusement les œuvres en projection ont un caractère « spectaculaire » qui se rapproche du cinéma populaire et particulièrement hollywoodien.

Leurs interrogations critiques de cette culture appartiennent cependant aux investigations du cinéma expérimental et alternatif.

Timelength invite le visiteur à s'engager dans un rapport frontal avec l'œuvre. Le choix de ne pas inclure de projections multi-écran est délibéré. C'est un moyen de regarder de plus près le rapport à l'image fixe et au pictural que ce type de projection suggère. En « exposant » l'image animée elle s'inscrit dans l'historique de l'exposition si longtemps marquée par l'image fixe, voire le tableau. En outre la lenteur qu'accusent les œuvres, leur quasi-fixité qui fait allonger le temps et qui les transforme en œuvres-durée joue intensément de ce lien contemplatif avec l'image fixe du tableau. Il ne s'agit pas d'assimiler le cinéma d'exposition au continuum pictural – sans aucun doute il le bouleverse – mais plutôt de voir « ce que signifie et comment se manifeste la réversion du mobile dans l'immobile »[4]. De fait, on espère que *Timelength* contribuera à remettre en question l'identité même de toute image, sa précarité, qu'elle soit fixe et possède un support matériel substantiel comme un tableau ou mobile et immatérielle comme dans une projection[5].

Si le rapport du visiteur avec les œuvres de *Timelength* est frontal il n'est pas pour autant nécessairement immobile. Malgré des séances de projections prédéterminées et un visionnement qui exige de la part du spectateur un arrêt calculé, les films de Snow et de de Rijke / de Rooij créent un espace dans la semi-obscurité, qui une fois le projecteur éteint, devient le lieu d'une mobilité scrutatrice. Dans les projections murales des vidéos de Grandmaison, MacGregor et Robert, on peut bien sûr se déplacer à sa guise puisqu'on est effectivement plus immobilisé devant l'image comme au cinéma. La question de la radicalité d'une œuvre dans le discours sur le cinéma d'exposition est soulevée en fonction de la mobilité du visiteur dans son rapport à l'image en mouvement. Cependant, faire une équivalence entre mobilité, liberté et radicalité d'un côté et immobilité, passivité et conventionnalisme de l'autre est simplifier la problématique de réception des œuvres d'art ; c'est gommer une multitude d'autres facteurs qui influent sur la réception des œuvres[6]. Il est donc beaucoup plus productif d'entrevoir l'avènement de l'image animée et projetée (et aussi celui des pratiques sensorielles et non optiques) dans les musées et autres aires d'exposition comme un moyen de repenser les tensions qui se jouent toujours entre le spectateur ou le visiteur et une œuvre quelle qu'elle soit. C'est ainsi que l'on peut faire participer les modes de réception dits « conventionnels » au discours de la contemporanéité.

En fin de texte j'aimerais évoquer la pratique de la lecture (de récits fictifs particulièrement) comme pouvant ouvrir une brèche dans le discours du spectaculaire cinématique et comme pouvant faire réfléchir autrement à ce qui est en vue (et à l'écoute). La lecture est aussi une pratique marquée distinctement par la durée, elle nous astreint à des durées spécifiques. C'est dans l'effet d'absorption de l'esprit et du corps dans la lecture du récit et du décalage temporel qu'elle occasionne, dans la coupure qui s'ensuit d'avec le monde, et dans la nature intime et concentrée de cet envahissement qui active notre imaginaire, notre perception et nos sens, et oblige à un ajustement constant avec la réalité, que l'expérience de la lecture s'imbrique dans la mouvance réglée des images illuminées que le visiteur regarde dans l'obscurité.

NOTES

1. Raymond Bellour,« La querelle des dispositifs », *Art press* n° 262 (nov. 2000), p. 52. Un exemple parmi tant d'autres de cette « esthétique de la confusion » est la présentation de projections vidéo dans un espace cinéma avec aire de projection fermée et rangées de sièges minutieusement recréées pour l'occasion. On pense ici, entre autres, a *The Paradise Institute* de Janet Cardiff et George Bures Miller.
2. Philip Monk, « Paint it Black: Curating the Temporal Image », *Prefix*, n° 9 (May 2004), p. 17-18.
3. Michael Snow, « Please Take the Time to Read All of This », 2004. Commentaire reproduit dans ce catalogue, p. 99.
4. Jean-Christophe Royoux, « Cinéma d'exposition : l'espacement de la durée », *Art press* no. 262 (nov. 2000), p. 38.
5. Boris Groys, « On the Aesthetics of video installations » *Stan Douglas : Le Détroit*, catalogue d'exposition, Basel, Kunsthalle Basel, 2000.
6. Mark Nash, « Art and Cinema: Some Critical Reflections », *Documenta 11, Platform V: Exhibition Catalogue*, Ostfildern (Ruit), Hatje Cantz Publishers, 2002, p. 129-133.

BIOGRAPHIES

JEROEN DE RIJKE and WILLEM DE ROOIJ make 35 and 16 mm films and photographs. Their films however are presented solely in exhibition spaces and not theaters. They produce images whose subtle deployment transforms them into mental constructs that delve into the recesses of reality and meaning. De Rijke and de Rooij have been working and exhibiting together since 1994. They have had solo shows at The ICA (London), The Douglas Hyde Gallery (Dublin), Regen Projects (Los Angeles) and Kunsthalle (Zurich). They were nominated for The Hugo Boss Prize 2004. De Rijke and de Rooij live in Amsterdam and are represented by Galerie Daniel Buchholz in Cologne.

PASCAL GRANDMAISON uses video and photography to create images within a contemplative and durational framework. He has had solo exhibitions in Canada and abroad (Lyon and New York) and has been included in the group exhibition *Soundtrack,* which toured Canada. His work in video has been presented in festivals and biennials in Canada, Italy, England, Portugal and Switzerland. Pascal Grandmaison lives in Montreal. He is represented by Galerie René Blouin in Montreal.

STEFAN JOVANOVIČ is an artist and scholar. He has lectured in Film Studies at Concordia University and is currently pursuing a doctorate in art history at Université de Montréal. His dissertation research focuses on the incorporation of film and moving images into recent art practices. His most recently completed film is entitled *Cosmography* (2003). Stefan Jovanovič lives in Montreal.

GWEN MCGREGOR makes photographs and videos that explore the intricate structure of the mundane and the familiar. She has had solo shows at The Art Gallery of Ontario (Toronto), La Centrale (Montreal) and Ex Teresa Art Actual (Mexico City). Group exhibitions include The Nunnery Gallery in London, England and the York Quay Gallery in Toronto. She has received numerous grants from The Canada Council, Ontario Arts

Council and the Toronto Arts Council including the Canada Council New York studio. In 2003 she received the Friends of the Visual Arts Award given to one Toronto artist each year. Gwen MacGregor lives in Toronto and is represented by Jessica Bradley Art and Projects in Toronto.

JOCELYN ROBERT works in audio, computer, performance, installation, video and as a writer. Robert is particularly interested in exploring the subtle relationships that exist between sound, text and the visual. His works have been shown in Canada, the United States, Mexico, Chili, Australia and Europe. He has done solo performances and in collaboration with Diane Landry, Laetitia Sonami and Bruit TTV. He has realized installations with Émile Morin. He has produced cds in solo and more than twenty in collaboration with other artists. In 1993 he founded the artist run center Avatar in Québec City. He has participated in several artist in residence programs. He has been the recipient of numerous grants and in 2002 his video installation *L'Invention des animaux* was awarded the First Prize ex aequo, in the section *New Image* of the *Transmedial Festival* in Berlin. He lives in Québec City.

MICHAEL SNOW works in film, photography, holography, video, audio, installation, sculpture, painting and drawing. He also writes and has been a professional musician since the 1950s performing free improvisation and making numerous recordings. His work is broadly collected and he has had major solo exhibitions at the National Gallery of Canada (Ottawa), The Hara Museum (Tokyo), the Museum of Modern Art (New York) and the Centre Georges Pompidou (Paris). His experimental film work is shown extensively in film festivals across the world. In 2002 *Anarchive 2: Digital Snow*, an interactive DVD-ROM was co-published by Anarchive, Paris and La Fondation Daniel Langlois, Montreal. *Triage* a recently completed two-screen collaboration with Toronto filmmaker Carl Brown was shown at MOMA in New York. Michael Snow lives in Toronto and is represented by the Moore Gallery and The Jack Shainman Gallery in New York. His films are distributed by CFMDC in Toronto, Canyon Cinema and the New York Filmmakers Coop in the United States and Lux, Lightcone and Freunde der Deutschen Kinematek in Europe.

MICHÈLE THÉRIAULT is a curator, writer and editor. She has produced numerous exhibitions investigating a diversity of issues in the work of Canadian and international artists. Her articles and essays have appeared in exhibition catalogues, thematic anthologies and books, and in art and critical theory periodicals in Québec, Canada and Europe. From 1988 to

1996 she was a curator of contemporary art at the Art Gallery of Ontario in Toronto. She is Director of The Leonard & Bina Ellen Art Gallery of Concordia University and an Adjunct Professor to the Department of Studio Arts.

ANDY WARHOL died in New York in 1987 but his presence marks modern life and is still strongly felt in the public imagination. The ultimate Pop artist he produced paintings, prints, objects, films and a culture, which transformed artmaking into a social process and overturned notions of authorship and authenticity. Warhol's filmmaking activity began in the early 60s and came to a halt in 1972 when he pulled all his films from circulation. In 1982 Warhol allowed the Whitney Museum in collaboration with the Museum of Modern Art to retrieve his films and restore them. Funded by the Andy Warhol Foundation for the Visual Arts, The Andy Warhol Film Project was created to research and eventually make the films available for presentation. Warhol produced a series of 500 black and white *Screen Tests* between 1963 and 1966.

LIST OF WORKS

LISTES DES OEUVRES

JEROEN DE RIJKE and **WILLEM DE ROOIJ**
Bantar Gebang, 2000
35 mm color film with optical sound, 10 min.
Film 35 mm en couleur avec son optique, 10 min

Courtesy Daniel Buchholz Gallery, Cologne
Avec l'aimable concours de la Galerie Daniel Buchholz, Cologne

PASCAL GRANDMAISON
Spin, 2002
Looped DVD projection, 16 min.
Projection DVD en boucle, 16 min

Courtesy Galerie René Blouin, Montréal
Avec l'aimable concours de la Galerie René Blouin, Montréal

GWEN MCGREGOR
Up to the 8th floor, 2004
Triptych. Looped DVD projection
Triptyque. Projection DVD en boucle

JOCELYN ROBERT
Catarina, 2002
Looped DVD projection with sound, 9 min.
Projection DVD en boucle avec son, 9 min

MICHAEL SNOW
One Second in Montreal, 1969
16 mm black and white film, 26 min.
Film 16 mm en noir et blanc, 26 min

Side Seat Slides Paintings Sound Film, 1970
16 mm colour film with sound, 20 min.
Film 16 mm en couleur avec son, 20 min

See You Later / Au revoir, 1990
16 mm colour film with sound, 18 min.
Film 16 mm en couleur avec son, 18 min

Michael Snow's films are distributed by the Canadian Filmmakers Distribution Centre, Toronto / Les films de Michael Snow sont distribués par le Canadian Filmmakers Distribution Centre, Toronto

ANDY WARHOL
Screen Tests, 1963 - 1966
16 mm black and white film transferred to DVD, 4 min., each at 16 frames per second / Film 16 mm noir et blanc transféré sur DVD ; durée: 4 min, 16 plans seconde

Collection of The Andy Warhol Museum, Pittsburg / Collection du Andy Warhol Museum, Pittsburg

Screen Test: John Giorno, 1963
Screen Test: Ann Buchanan, 1964
Screen Test: Walter Dainwood, 1964
Screen Test: Billy Name, 1964
Screen Test: Lucinda Childs, 1964
Screen Test: Donyale Luna, 1965
Screen Test: Marcel Duchamp, 1966

Off site screening / Présentation hors les murs
La Sala Rossa, 4848, boul. Saint-Laurent
December 12th / 12 décembre 16h.

Empire, 1964
16mm black and white film, 444 min. 26 sec., 18 frames per second
Film 16mm noir et blanc ; durée : 444 min 26 s, 18 plans seconde

Collection of the Museum of Modern Art, Circulating Film & Video Library, New York / Collection du Museum of Modern Art, Circulating Film & Video Library, New York

This publication was made possible by the financial support provided by the Canada Council, the Iris Westerberg Stern Fund and the Friends of the Gallery.

Cette publication a été réalisée grâce à l'appui financier du Conseil des Arts du Canada, du Fonds Iris Westerberg Stern et des Amis de la Galerie.

Timelength : de Rijke / de Rooij, Pascal Grandmaison, Gwen MacGregor, Jocelyn Robert, Michael Snow, Andy Warhol
Exhibition presented from November 11 to December 22, 2004 / Exposition présentée du 11 novembre au 22 décembre 2004.

Curator / Commissaire : Michèle Thériault
Production : Galerie Leonard & Bina Ellen, Université Concordia

Publication
Coordination / Coordination de la publication : Michèle Thériault
Essays / Essais : Stefan Jovanovič, Michèle Thériault
Additional Texts / Textes complémentaires : Michèle Thériault
Editing / Révision : Lucie Chevalier (français), Paddy O'Brien (English)
Proofreading / Correction d'épreuves : Michèle Thériault, Lucie Chevalier
English Translation / Traduction vers l'anglais : Donald McGrath, Michèle Thériault
French Translation / Traduction vers le français : Lucie Chevalier
Design / Graphisme : Uniform
Printing / Impression : L'Empreinte

Staff / Personnel
Direction : Michèle Thériault
Max Stern Curator of the Permanent Collection / Conservatrice Max Stern de la collection permanente : Nathalie Garneau
Education Coordinator / Coordinatrice à l'éducation : Piera Palucci
Curatorial Assistant / Adjoint à la conservation : John Latour
Technical Coordinator / Direction technique : Luigi Discenza
Administrative Assistant / Adjointe administrative : Vanessa Herrick
Office assistance / Soutien administratif : Doreen Wittenbols

Dépôt legal – Bibliothèque nationale du Canada, 2004
Dépôt legal – Bibliothèque nationale du Québec, 2004

Galerie Leonard & Bina Ellen Art Gallery
Concordia University
1400, boul. de Maisonneuve ouest, LB 165
Montréal (Québec) H3G 1M8
514-848-2424 poste 4750
ellengal@alcor.concordia.ca

ISBN 2-920394-63-0

Photo Credits / Crédits photographiques
Works / Œuvres
Jeroen de Rijke / Willem de Rooij : Galerie Daniel Buchholz, Cologne
Pascal Grandmaison : Pascal Grandmaison
Gwen MacGregor : Gwen MacGregor
Jocelyn Robert : Jocelyn Robert
Michael Snow : Michael Snow + Canadian Filmmakers Distribution Centre, Toronto
Andy Warhol : The Andy Warhol Museum, Pittsburg
Images of an itinerary / Parcours en images
Denis Farley

Acknowledgements / Remerciements
This exhibition was made possible by the expertise of Cindy Canavan and Nisan Greenidge, IITS, and by the assistance of Philippe Spurrell of Circus Maximus and of Dazibao. I am indebted to the Gallery's staff for their support and to Luigi Discenza, technical coordinator, for his tireless dedication to the project assisted by Oscar Varese, Barry Allikas, Duncan Chisholm and Michael Merrill. The presentation of Andy Warhol's film *Empire* was Piera Palucci's wonderful initiative. From the outset all of the artists supported the project enthusiastically, and it is the singular nature of their work that allowed me to give shape to my thoughts.

L'exposition a bénéficié de l'expertise de Cindy Canavan et de Nisan Greenidge, IITS, ainsi que de la précieuse collaboration de Philippe Spurrell de Circus Maximus et de Dazibao. Je tiens à remercier vivement le personnel de la Galerie et à souligner le dévouement tout particulier de Luigi Discenza à la direction technique et des techniciens Oscar Varese, Michael Merrill, Duncan Chisholm et Barry Allikas. L'excellente idée de présenter le film *Empire* de Andy Warhol est venue de Piera Palucci. Tous les artistes ont dès le départ appuyé avec enthousiasme le projet et c'est la singularité de leur œuvre qui a permis à ma réflexion de porter fruit.

Concordia
UNIVERSITY

Conseil des Arts du Canada
Canada Council for the Arts